D1320048

WHO WILL DELIVER US?

PAUL F.M. ZAHL

WHO WILL DELIVER US?

The Present Power of the Death of Christ

WIPF & STOCK · Eugene, Oregon

Wipf and Stock Publishers
199 W 8th Ave, Suite 3
Eugene, OR 97401

Who Will Deliver Us?
The Present Power of the Death of Christ
By Zahl, Paul F. M.
Copyright©1983 by Zahl, Paul F. M.
ISBN 13: 978-1-60608-212-6
Publication date 10/08/2008
Previously published by Seabury Press, 1983

To
John Ford
and
Fitz Allison

Contents

Preface

SEVERAL years ago, I heard for what seemed like the first time the good news of the Christian faith. In a period when I was overcome by feelings of depression, self-pity, and rage, a religious response to my condition was held out to me. The good news I heard helped to lift the depression, sufficed to disarm the self-pity, and became an antidote to the rage. Over a few months, my desperate feelings were transformed into a mood of hope and actual joy. As the evangelical subculture I entered would have said, I "became a Christian." So far as it goes, the phrase accurately describes what happened. Old words and ancient symbols of religion crossed over from the world of abstraction to vivid pertinence for my own struggles.

What actually happened? At the time, I was not able to explain except in borrowed phrases. Today I am trying to say. The experience had something to do with a steady hand reaching down to lift me out of a hole. It felt as simple as being loved in my frailty and my willfulness. It was not primarily a question of intellectual conviction. It was rather a question of appreciating that my weakness, as well as my meanness of spirit, could be regarded with compassion by another. Such compassion was embodied partly in the believers who first cared for me then. But the governing symbol of the compassion was identified, in ways closer to feelings than to words, with the old story of the cross of Jesus Christ. The governing symbol was the cross.

From one point of view, an earthquake had happened. The aftereffects of the earthquake included two years of study in England, ordination to the ministry of the Episcopal Church, and the beginnings of my own marriage and family. From another point of view, it was a tiny step. The cross, governing symbol of my faith, carried great emotion for me, but it was also enveloped in mist. I would have told anyone who asked that the heartbeat of Christianity is the cross of Jesus Christ. Yet I did not understand and could not explain how it might be that one man's dying in ancient times could make a perceived difference to a sufferer—to anyone, for that matter—in present experience.

Traditionally, Christian theology has described what happened when Jesus died as an atonement. What was formerly divided is now "at one." Theology has reckoned that a great divide exists between God and humanity and that our experience of tragedy, which casts a long shadow over the whole world, is to a large extent the result of such a divide. For the divide to be bridged, reconciliation needs to take place. The cross represents this reconciliation. Classically, the meaning of the cross is expressed in the words "Christ died for our sins."

For me the meaning of these words began to become clear several years after I embraced Christianity. It was as though I had grasped at the outset only a fraction of the Christian message. Their impact came home later, when I was undeniably at the mercy of forces within myself that robbed me of even the appearance of freedom. Nowhere were the words received more clearly than in the misery of my own anxiety and depression. To put it another way, the good news of Christianity rang true at a point when there was no escaping the fact that my life was out of control.

I offer this book in the hope of sharing what I have learned about the blood of Christ. It is sadly true that many people experience life, in their own ways and to differing degrees, as a prison. Prisons can be made of impossible circumstances outside a person, driving compulsions and fears inside, or a mixture of both. Many of us are cowed by life. The person who seems strong on the outside may be masking painful feelings of fragility. The person who seems self-effacing at first may be obsessed by resentment and revenge. Adding to the burden of our personal pain is the tragic perception that the whole world is filled with terror and tragedy, striking down innocent people in the thousands and even millions through war and disaster. Even here, the fact that Christ died for our sins, that atonement was made between God and humanity, is of stunning, specific application to the universal drama of pain and sorrow. The atonement carries meaning to our individual personal lives, to the lives of our families and communities, and to the life of the whole world.

I believe in the atonement and offer this book in the confidence that Christ's "death for our sins" may give to many lives a renewed basis for hope within a world broken on the wheel of pain, sorrow, and depression.

Introduction:
Redeeming the Message

"CHRIST died for our sins." The words are familiar — almost too familiar. Do they convey a message of reassurance? Or do they summon the image of a crudely painted sign planted along a country road? Words have associations. These five words, in particular, have bad associations. They are haunted by specters of bigotry, ignorance, and self-righteousness.

There is tragic irony in this. A crucial idea is almost lost to us because the words for it are tarnished. Yet my life has turned on these tarnished words.

These five words, "Christ died for our sins," express a conviction. They voice a confidence that atonement has been made for the whole history of injustice suffered by the human race. What is atonement? Atonement is action carried out to make up for injustice. For example, a young woman is convinced that she is responsible for her lover's suicide. She devotes the next ten years of her life to an organization that helps desperate people. In her mind, these years are atonement for the part she played in a tragedy she cannot forget. Even though her lover is dead, she answers to his accusing memory, which lives on inside her mind. Whenever we try to compensate

5

someone for damages we think are our fault, we are trying to make atonement.

In Christian theology, atonement is what Jesus Christ did on the cross. God, says the Bible, was wounded by humanity's disobedience. The poetic setting of this disobedience was the Garden of Eden. The act, however, was and is universal, taking place through all times and cultures of the human race. God is wounded. He seeks to bring us back to him. But we fear him and we flee. To bring us together, atonement must be made. The old story says that Jesus Christ, in his death on the cross, is our atonement.

Three terms related to atonement need to be defined from the start. The first is the Law. *Law* with a capital *L* refers to the moral precepts of the Old Testament, as symbolized and summarized in the Ten Commandments, the Law given to Moses. This is the Law from God, understood as a set of revealed ideals for true religion and just relationships. In comparison, *law* with a small *l* refers to an interior principle of demand or *ought* that seems universal in human nature. In this sense, law is any voice that makes us feel we *must* do something or be something to merit the approval of another. For example, what we shall call the "law of capability" is the demand a person may feel that he be 100 percent capable in everything he does—or else! In the Bible the Law comes from God; in daily living law is an internalized principle of self-accusation. We might say that the innumerable laws we carry inside us are bastard children of the Law.

A second term that requires definition is *justification by faith*. This term can be explained from its use in the art of printing. If a line of type is out of alignment, it needs to be "justified," that is, moved so as to be in line with the type above and below it. In theology, justification means to be reconciled to God so that we are not adversaries but live in harmony. In the New Testament, justification occurs by faith (trusting God) rather than by performance (sheer adequacy) because we could never do enough to earn it.

A third word needs definition. This is *imputation*. *To impute* means to ascribe a characteristic to someone that he does not have by nature. For example, I can, for any number of reasons, impute integrity to someone I normally think of as corrupt, or deviousness to someone I normally think of as decent. In doing so I may actually affect the person's behavior. *A person can become as he is regarded*. We can "rise" to fit someone's inflated impression of us, or "fall" to bear out his worst suspicions. The person who regards us positively or negatively holds, in either case, enormous power over us. In the Bible, God's power to impute becomes an instrument of awesome influence for good. "Happy is the one to whom the Lord imputes no guilt" (Ps. 32:2).

"Christ died for our sins" is a conviction of immense potential personal significance. Like planets orbiting the sun, words like *atonement, Law, law, justification by faith*, and *imputation* comprise a system of ideas that reflects this conviction. They are a lens through which we may more clearly see Christianity's central concerns. They are an avenue by which we may approach the core of Christian faith. They are a door through which I, for one, have been able to enter.

They are not a new thing. They are ancient ideas. They were at the heart of Saint Paul's interpretation of Jesus. They were crucial for Saint Augustine as he pondered a shattering world order almost four hundred years later. They were the flame that lit the Protestant Reformation, in particular the theology of Martin Luther. They were the motive force behind John Wesley and the Great Awakening of the eighteenth century. They were the soul of Karl Barth's summons to the church in the early part of this century.

In the past, the doctrines of atonement and justification by faith have proven to be catalysts for reform and renewal in the Christian community. In recent years they have been neglected in the mainstream of church life, left for the most part as a province of beleaguered evangelicals. They have been incriminated by keeping bad company. But the ideas themselves are not dead. They may be hidden behind ancient words, but they can live again. They can work for us in the midst of life. That Christ died for our sins may yet be a conviction capable of bursting through the years and changes into the most closely guarded prisons of the human heart.

I

The Dereliction
of Fear

AN old joke is repeated year after year in the graffiti on public buildings. Someone writes for all to see, "Christ is the answer." After it someone has added, "But what is the question?" The addition is perceptive. Unless Christ is a response to a question we are really asking, it makes no sense to say that he is the answer. If there is no question, an answer is written on the wind.

Is there a real problem to which the atonement of Jesus Christ offers a solution? What is irremediable about the human condition that it should require a death for healing to occur? The extreme nature of the solution, one person's death for the "salvation" of others, presupposes an extreme need on the part of the others. Does such a need exist? Is it that extreme?

In responding to these questions, we can start by considering some everyday problems of living, in order to discover the needs and intentions which give rise to them. Consider the problem of stress. Stress is pressure caused by the convergence of strong, conflicting claims upon the self. If, for example, a person feels under the pressure of having to perform at peak efficiency in his work at all times, and also desires to

9

be an attentive partner to his spouse and present parent to his children, he will almost certainly experience stress. How can he balance the strong, conflicting claims upon his time? Add to them his desire to have time for his own interests, and he will have a very hard time reconciling the demands. This is a type of stress that is familiar to many of us.

It is all the worse in a period like the present, when the law of capability is in force. This is the law that judges us wanting if we are not capable, if we cannot handle it *all*, if we are not competent to balance our diverse commitments without a slip. Who among us does not live under the dread sign of the law of capability?

In a commencement address, the columnist Ellen Goodman once described the Model Woman of today, somewhat along the following lines. She gets up at six-thirty in the morning and jogs five miles. At seven-thirty she cooks a totally nourishing breakfast for her husband and two beautiful children. By eight-thirty the children have left for school, her husband to his office, and she is on the way to her incredibly demanding job: she is advertising director for a major firm. All day long she attends meetings and makes important decisions. When she finally arrives home, it is quite late because she had to attend a board meeting for a community-service organization of which she is chairman. But she does not get home too late to fix her children a totally nourishing supper. She helps both of them with their homework and has meaningful goodnights with each. Yet she still has time to plug in the Cuisinart to prepare a gourmet, candlelit supper for herself and her husband. As the day comes to an end, the Model Woman has a totally fulfilling yet deeply honest sexual relationship with her admirably sensitive husband.

Under the law of capability the Model Woman, like any of us, is bound to sicken. We are all simply human. Stress, which takes innumerable forms in our lives and of which the law of capability is one, results from strong, conflicting claims upon the self. Ultimately, stress involves a religious problem. The problem underlying our need to reconcile conflicting demands is this: What establishes my identity? What *is* my identity?

Many of us act as if the answer to this question were performance. If I can do enough of the right things, I will have established my worth. Identity is the sum of my achievements. Hence, if I can satisfy the boss, meet the needs of my spouse and children, and still do justice to my inner aspirations, then I will have proven my worth. There are infinite ways to prove our worth along these lines. The basic equation is this: I am what I do. It is a religious position in life because it tries to answer in practical terms the question, Who am I and what is my niche in the universe? On this reading, my niche is in proportion to my deeds. In Christian theology, such a position is called justification by works. It assumes that my worth is measured by my performance. Conversely, it conceals, thinly, a dark and ghastly fear: If I do not perform, I will be judged unworthy. To myself I will cease to exist.

The vitiating effects of stress in everyday life are well known: fatigue, bad temper, depression, and occasionally, if escape valves cannot be found from time to time, violent reaction. Stress is an everyday tragedy that makes many of us become unhappy, resentful people. One of the unhappiest people I know is a man who by his forty-fifth birthday had risen to the height of the legal profession. His achievements appeared enviable, although in recent years he looked tired. Not long ago he turned to his wife and asked her for a divorce. He said he wanted to live, to cut loose from his imprisoning obligations. And he has cut loose. How much has he lost? His wife? His children? The children say they cannot forgive him. They ask, "Why didn't you ever tell Mom, or at least us, that something was wrong? We knew you were miserable. Why did you never say so?"

Family tragedy is often a result of stress. If stress is not relieved in a person, it becomes tinder for an explosion. The person who is feeling the stress rarely lets us know directly until he is past a point of no return. The rest of us are almost always shocked when the explosion comes.

One way of describing stress is to picture a vise in a tool-room. One arm of the vise represents obligation or law, the force of *ought*. The opposing arm of the vise represents "what I want and what I need." Human beings are held in this vise, squeezed there by inexorable, opposing forces. Is it possible to escape?

The vise is so strong because our fear is so great. In fact, the power of the vise to crush is in proportion to our fear. If we did not fear the judgment of the *ought*, it would hold no power over us. Instead, we believe with passionate intensity that if we should fail in fulfilling the requirements we believe are placed on us by others for the sake of achieving their favor, then we will have nothing at all. If we fail, we shall amount to nothing, we shall *be* nothing. Such a destiny is completely unacceptable. So we accept grudgingly the yoke of law, that we may strive to win the favor of the others whom we allow to carry our value. We allow others to tell us how much we are worth.

Stress is a common experience of life from which we are in urgent need of relief. Another common affliction, often related to stress, is depression. Depression is a heavy cloud of hopelessness settling over our confidence and hope. It is often brought on by an event that touches a hopeless part of us—we might say, the hopeless person who lives inside us. In some of us, this hopeless self holds sway over the rest of the self. We can suddenly be depleted of confidence by the conviction that we can never attain the affirmation that seems so necessary for us to live and breathe. When I myself become depressed, it is usually through the gateway of someone else's judgment as I perceive it. According to this judgment, I feel my own weakness so heavily that it seems to express the whole truth about my life. It becomes all I believe about myself. We can be so taken over by depression that we cannot drive a car or read a book or talk to our spouse or fix a meal. Life literally stops. No reason in the world can convince us that we should put one foot in front of the other.

Depression is a significant clue to our need for value to be assigned us. In the presence of condemnation, which signals the absence of positive value, we wilt to nothing. This wilting to nothing is something we all fear. Depression is a prison cell. Once we are inside its four walls, we can envisage no escape.

Whatever cure may exist for depression, such a cure must be able to fulfill our need for value. Such a cure will need to minister to the hidden fear that inwardly we are diminished and impotent, desperate for a sense of worth and suspecting the worst about ourselves.

A third clue to our fragility and fear is the universal, driving emotion of anger. It is as universal as the air we breathe and sets the stage for war and inhumanity on a sickening scale. We can define anger at its root as a response to hostile invasions of the self. We say, "He is an angry person"; we mean that he is always taking offense. He lives as though everyone is out to get him. Anger is like the old advice about defensive driving: Drive as if all the other drivers hate you and are trying to kill you. Anger is a land mine inside us: a tremor can set it off. An angry person is likely to interpret exchanges with other people as attacks upon himself. Even if we are "right" in our anger, that is, even if we are actually being attacked and are only defending ourselves, nevertheless the intensity of our anger, the red lights going on and off, the racing heartbeat, our hands shaking, suggest something arising from the hidden, anxious parts of us. Behind the pattern of our rage lies a most painful insecurity.

At the root of anger is fear. So deeply ingrained is the belief that we are small and weak, so vulnerable do we actually feel, that we have to protect ourselves with all our might. Anger is instinctive protection in the face of assault. It is hot and long-lasting to the degree that it masks perceived weakness. It is not a response from strength, it is a response from weakness.

Anger is a heavy burden. It can make daily life into a hell. It festers and seems intractable. Anger, like stress and depression, is a prison from which few of us escape.

The conditions of stress, depression, and anger are connected to many other, corollary conditions. The fears that lie beneath them extend to all humanity and spawn millions of children: symptoms, sorrows, and worries. These are not private matters. They are not solitary affairs of the psyche carried on behind closed shutters of the mind and heart. No, they have consequences. Stress reproduced arithmetically in individuals becomes a culture that is squeezed by stress. You can feel the stress of a family, a community, or a city. Just spend time with a family before one of the children is to be married. The tension emanating from an anxious father or mother or from the child himself spreads out like the spokes of a wheel. The more frantic and consuming the wedding preparations, the more volatile may be the tensions simmering below the surface. The whole family may be in agony, and the most casual visitor picks it up.

You can feel the stress of a city. New York City, for example, communicates stress to its people and picks it up from them. Nobody knows which happens first: Different kinds of stress have become mixed together. The result is stress in the city on a large scale. It contaminates. Is it not possible to feel the stress of a whole country? If you had been in England during the 1981 race riots in London and Liverpool, you would have felt the tension and fear all around you. Everywhere, emanating from almost everyone was the sense of shock that "this could happen here." Stress and the fear behind it had become a national phenomenon.

All this indicates that afflicting life problems such as stress, depression, and anger are not a private matter. They reproduce themselves in people so as to affect the moods and actions of communities. The earth is filled with their effects. We hear of "a shot heard round the world" and know what it means. An angry action, "justified" or "unjustified," touches off others. We hear of "epidemics of crime." A person is pushed off a subway platform in the face of an oncoming train, then it happens eight times in one week. A nun is raped, then a city has a rash of assaults on clergy. Like crime, anger can be caught and flare up. Even depression can be caught. We know what it is to breathe an atmosphere of depression. We can walk into a room and find ourselves depressed by the depression of the people in it. We speak of a community in which no one has work as "depressed." Loss of hope can touch a whole environment. Diseases of the self impinge upon the world. It is possible to deduce that the long chronicle of "man's inhumanity to man" has roots in an aggregate of personal imprisonments from fear that bind everyone who has ever been born.

Can we illuminate further this tragic wound of fear, because of which so much of the world's suffering is rooted in the very nature of being human? The fear, I believe, has to do with what philosophy might term an anxiety of nonbeing. It is the feeling that we are, according to a convincing inner imprint, exposed and vulnerable persons, weak in the extreme, unable to protect ourselves by ourselves. Whether this feeling reflects memories from birth or childhood, or the sheer fact that human beings require the care and protection of their parents longer than any other animal species, or collective memories of pain passed down by means of heredity and intensified over the centuries, is not something we can know with any certainty. The question of the root of humanity's fear, like the ultimate, parallel question of the root of evil, cannot be answered —certainly not to the satisfaction of countless human beings who have cause to raise their fists at the God who would allow such suffering to disease their lives. And this is not to mention the random evils of life, like plagues, accidents, and natural disasters. They appear blankly meaningless. Random evil will be considered later, in the chapter on innocent affliction. But we need to ask now and ask urgently, What is the origin of fear? The question is all the more urgent if the atonement of Jesus Christ on the cross is to make any sense as a possible remedy.

From the standpoint of the New Testament, the principal cause of fear is punishment. "Fear has to do with punishment" (1 John 4:18). For the Jews, to use Saint Paul's frame of reference, fear has to do with God's judgment of a person's or people's failure to live up to the standards of the Law, symbolized and summarized in the Ten Commandments. For the non-Jew, fear has to do with terror of the fateful, nameless forces that dominate humanity and nature, of which idols must be built and to which tribute must be paid. "Formerly, when you did not know God, you were in bondage to beings that by nature are no gods . . . to the elemental spirits" (Gal. 4:8-9).

For non-Jews, according to Paul, there is another fear as well, fear of violating the natural conscience implanted in all persons, the "law written on the heart." This is a universal, indwelling principle of right and wrong, which is comparable to the more informed Law revealed to the Jews. Whether a person is Jew or Gentile, fear at its root is fear of God or forces conceived to be God. Even the Gentiles who stand helpless before their idols are answering unconsciously to God. They know there is something to fear. Their manufactured names and images for various gods are untrue ways of imaging the face of judgment that in fact really exists, which the Jews know as the God who gave the Law.

According to Paul, as he comments on the tragic cycles of human history, the primary fact for us to reckon with is the judgment we face, regardless of whether we identify this as coming from the God of the Jews or from universal cosmic forces. For Paul the fear of judgment represented in the idols of Gentile religion manifests the unconscious accountability of all humanity to ultimate judgment, judgment that Paul believes originates from one living God. Paul envisions all humanity without exception as answerable to a judge: "All who have sinned without the Law will also perish without the Law, and all who have sinned under the Law will be judged by the Law . . . God shows no partiality" (Rom. 2:12, 11).

I am suggesting that the fear beneath all fears, which in turn creates the stress, depression, and anger of everyday life and human history, is fear of ultimate judgment. This is to say, the fear of ultimate condemnation, because fear of judgment implies condemnation. If we were confident of acquittal, judgment would not possess the sting it does. Judgment for us entails condemnation. And condemnation spells a loss of status and position that in turn connotes a radical diminishing of the self, to the point of nonbeing. Do we not all recognize the chilling voice of condemnation when it comes from quarters to which we have given power? Can you recall the terror of being singled out as a child before a classroom of peers to be punished for a crime you actually did commit and for which you could offer absolutely no excuse? Have you ever gotten over the humiliation? Is there not a large element of humiliation in the experience of condemnation, which brings up acutely painful associations of shame and exposure? To draw again from Saint Paul, condemnation "stops the mouth of every man" (Rom. 3:19). It declares we haven't a leg to stand on. There is no *terra firma* in the court of condemnation. It would be better for us to be swallowed up and utterly forgotten.

Imprisonments of fear, rooted in an ultimate fear of condemnation, cause the experience of living to be colored by anxiety, tension, depression, and rage. We are not given to know the first cause of this fear. We do know that it seems to be a part of us all. Whether it is conditioned psychologically or implanted genetically or a mixture of both with any other factors, it motivates us in the interest of warding off threats of condemnation. We would do almost anything to prevent a return to the unbearable place of exposure, nonstatus, and dereliction to which condemnation refers us.

Will we do anything to prevent our return to that place? Will

we in fact go to any lengths to defend ourselves against condemnation? Is the fear of judgment so vitiating that we would
devote our entire lives to getting free of it? We are certainly
aware of lifelong strategies and patterns in us that *appear* to
draw their impressive energy from the need to liberate humanity from fear. If the problem of being human is at base a fear
of condemnation, then the historic challenge of being human
is to break free from fear. How can we do this?

One strategy that occurs naturally is flight. It seems obvious
that the wisest thing to do in the face of a gale wind is to get
out of the way as fast as possible. Our flight from judgment
can take many forms. Let's say that a man has become afraid
of his wife. Her sarcasm and angry undertone when she ad-
dresses him, made worse by the sharp perceptiveness with
which she "sees through him," have become so wounding with
the passage of time that he must avoid direct encounter as best
he can. His pattern is to busy himself single-mindedly, when
he is home, with the children. The children do in fact need
him, and his wife can definitely use the help. But that is not
why he devotes himself so fully to them. He is using them as
a screen against his wife. Unfortunately, he is unaware that
the edge to his wife's conversation, her sarcasm and criticism,
are a way of pleading for recognition, her plea for him to actually face her and talk to her as one human being to another.
He does not realize that. What he hears from her is judgment.
So he flees, the children being his temporary place of refuge.

In such situations, intimacy connotes a much-feared encounter by which "if this person really knew what I am like,
she could not possibly love me." By definition, this "I" believes it is unlovable. Hence many possibilities of intimacy are
left untested because of the felt danger of condemnation. In the
case of the man who immerses himself in his children rather
than spend time with his wife, his wife has come, in his mind,
to embody condemnation. We will flee a relationship because
of the threat of judgment. We will flee by as many strategies
as there are people, but flee we must. The biblical prototype

of this is Adam's flight from God in Eden: "I heard your voice in the garden, and I was afraid, because I was naked; and I hid myself" (Gen. 3:10).

Fleeing from the threat of condemnation often involves a splitting of the self. We must remove ourselves from a threatening situation but cannot in every instance remove ourselves bodily. So our mind or a part of our mind splits off. Perhaps I am sitting down in conversation with a person whom I dislike. Talking with the person is agony for me. So my real attention moves elsewhere. I decide to think about my hobby or a person I wish were here or a blissful experience from the past or a hope for the future. I am "a million miles away." I am in flight. In fact, I am neither fully present nor fully absent: I am split. I enter the business of avoiding painful experiences by absenting my inner self, or as much of that self as I can get away with.

The problem with escape as a way of quieting our fear of condemnation is that it does not quiet the condemnation. It does not subdue the panicky belief that the universe is essentially hostile. When we come down from our chosen refuge to reality, it is the same. The problem has not gone away.

One fully effective route of escape is suicide. It is the only final, foolproof remedy for a life of fear. When a woman in her forties took her own life several years ago, her close friends were overcome with surprise. Why did she do it? No one really knew, but her friends were able to piece together information to explain her emotional state before she died. She had been a beautiful woman, a model in fact. Cancer, however, had been diagnosed, and the chemotherapy that was prescribed took a terrible toll on her beauty. We believe she never recovered from having to watch her hair fall out. When during a period of actual remission she was rejected by a former lover, she committed suicide. We could only conjecture what went through her mind. It was not the cancer as such that poisoned her desire to live, it was her fear of rejection on account of her vanished beauty. Her sense of worth was tied up in her appearance more closely than we had ever imagined. When her beauty vanished, she believed she had nothing. She took her own life.

Suicide includes more than just the death of the body. It is a method universally employed to root out experiences and memories of conflict. If a part of you causes you shame, you can cut it off. Origen, the early Christian theologian, castrated himself as a youth because he was frightened by the compulsion of his sexuality. If you have ever been hurt in love, and found yourself saying, "I will never get hurt again"—which probably means "I will never again invest myself in another person so as to leave myself open to such pain"—you may be voluntarily putting to death the part of you that can love unreservedly. We say, "Part of him died when such-and-such happened." In other words, the pain of a loss or defeat was so great that the hurt part went into hiding, or for all practical purposes agreed to die. Splitting of the self, which is an almost universal strategy of escape, implies practical suicide. As a form of escape, it is effective. It is also the heart and soul of tragedy.

A second, opposite strategy for containing our universal fear of condemnation is open resistance. This tactic requires anger at the condemnation, together with a conviction that it is unjust and ought to be fought. A celebrated spokesman for this second strategy is Job, who in his suffering contends with God: "Today, my complaint is bitter, his hand is heavy in spite of my groaning. Oh, that I knew where I might find him, that I might come even to his seat! I would lay my case before him and fill my mouth with arguments. I would learn what he would answer me, and understand what he would say to me. Would he contend with me in the greatness of his power? No, he would give heed to me. There an upright man could reason with him, and I should be acquitted forever by my judge" (Job 23:1-7).

The strategy of open resistance in the face of fear is a response of impressive courage. Because it requires both courage and conviction, qualities which can halt the opposition in their tracks, it is often a more effective strategy than escape. The self-confidence implicit in open resistance can light a fiery torch in face of the dark powers of condemnation. Open resistance is a tactic we can affirm because it scores successes. In daily living, examples of open resistance include the attempts of growing children to become separate from their parents, the domestic struggles in which men and women strive to become mutual partners in marriage, the fledgling independence of a young professional when he decides to ask for a raise, and so on. Anytime we sue for justice in what we believe is an unjust situation, we are going the way of open resistance.

Communities and peoples, like individuals, can resist openly. When we admire the intellectual aspirations of the Renaissance in western Europe, we are observing a parable of humanity's lifting up its head from the oppression of ignorance. A vivid picture of such aspirations is seen in the much-visited courtyard of Duke Humphrey's Library in Oxford, with its five orders of columns piled one on top of another, shooting straight up as if to heaven. The architecture is a Renaissance embodiment of humanity's resisting, throwing off centuries of intellectual and spiritual subjugation. Whatever form it takes, past or present, open resistance is a pathway of impressive courage.

The tragic flaw of open resistance is that it is seldom strong enough in itself to win decisive victory. Human feelings of condemnation, hence diminution, run deep. The symptoms they produce—whether stress, depression, anger, whatever—are so powerful in the aggregate, achieving such force as they are passed down through generations and history, that even the most heroic revolt against condemnation is inadequate to defeat them. I have in mind not only the long shadows of fear that exist within people, but also the leaden weight of institutions and historical forces that oppress races and nations. We have not, except in extremely limited situations, achieved an end to oppression. In this century, the humanistic hopes of

Western societies were denied fulfillment by the existence of just two horrible facts: the unbelievable loss of life in the trenches during World War I and the Holocaust of the Jews during World War II. The forces of oppression on the human spirit are too vile and deeply rooted to be put to death by the heroic tactic of open resistance.

A third strategy for resolving the problem of fear is the way of appeasement. This strategy recognizes the superior force of the judgment we face. It is aware of the shivering vulnerability we feel in our inner as well as our outer selves. This strategy attempts to negotiate for peace with the hostile powers of condemnation, hoping for the best. Its tragic flaw is the resentment that accompanies it. Think what goes on inside us when we say yes against our will. True, there are situations in which we are running scared. We conclude that we might lose a lot if we stand up to the opposing force and defend ourselves. Appeasement seems expedient. I think of a person sitting by his desk at the office. He feels pressured by the boss to complete a certain piece of work. Every time he is reminded—officiously, he thinks—about the deadline, he says, "Yes, sir, absolutely, it's coming right up." Before the authority he jumps through a hoop, and does it again and again. The trouble is, each time he jumps he gets more furious on the inside. Appeasement and resentment are close relations.

Appeasement is an attempt to take upon oneself the burden of another's judgment and thereby to disarm it. It means accepting the judgment as correct and bowing to it in the hope of withstanding it. It is undertaken as a means of making friends with it. Unfortunately, this never happens. As soon as we bow to a human being or institution in judgment over us, we are in their power. We will never be good enough to satisfy them. The law laid upon us and accepted by us is relentless. It cannot be satisfied.

I wonder if any of us are strong enough to withstand the perceived judgments upon our lives, which touch the fears within. Have you ever tried to win the favor of a person who actively dislikes you? To get him to like you, you may have changed your style of dress. You may have altered your schedule. You may have stopped something you've been doing, or started something new. You may have carried out his wishes to the last detail. You may have tried once, then again, then a thousand times. But you have not won from this person the affirmation you so deeply desire.

Judgment steamrolls over most of us. We observe, "All the life has gone out of that person." "She is a defeated person." "His last failure killed him." "He is a shadow of his former self." The nature of judgment is to be implacable. Appeasement, like anger and open resistance, manifests itself in the world of religion. We could almost say that the whole idea of sacrifice in religion is a child of appeasement. We fear a god, so we appease him by sacrificing something that is valuable to us: a goat or dove or young maiden or firstborn son. In the Old Testament, humanity sought to appease God by obeying the Law, satisfying his moral demands. Saint Paul, schooled in the Old Testament, made this a devoted way of life before his experience on the road to Damascus. He took out of his own hide what he understood to be God's eternal, utter demand for perfection. He wrote to the Philippians, "If any other man thinks he has reason for confidence in the flesh, I have more: circumcised on the eighth day, of the people of Israel, of the tribe of Benjamin, a Hebrew born of Hebrews; as to the Law a Pharisee . . . as to righteousness under the Law blameless" (Phil. 3:4-6). After trying to win the friendship of God, creator of the principle of law and demand, Paul concluded he had failed. He came to believe that he could never have won. He could not set out to appease God and succeed. The moral demand is too great. It cannot be met. And from the standpoint of another, different strategy for dealing with judgment, Paul closed the book on his past life of appeasement: "Whatever gain I once had, I now count as loss for the sake of Christ" (Phil. 3:7).

In the strategy of appeasement we are edging longingly

towards hope of an atonement. Atonement means sacrificing a valued possession in order to satisfy the judgment of a power to which we are accountable. It involves full payment of a claim on us. But there is a crucial difference between atonement and appeasement: Atonement suggests confidence on the part of the person who offers the sacrifice that the worth of the sacrifice corresponds in cost to the demand of the judge. For example, in Greek mythology Hercules undertook his Twelve Labors in the confidence that by completing them, he could atone for the murder of his wife and children. Appeasement, on the other hand, is degrading, because we know, when we appease, that it is only a temporary measure, offering a small part of what we actually owe. For example, the Munich Pact was an appeasement because it only *put off* Hitler's attack on Europe. Appeasement is a strategem to forestall but not vitiate the reckoning we fear. It is a stalling for time in the face of judgment that is irresistible and unquenchable. The tragedy of appeasement is that in the end, it always fails. Indeed, it serves to strengthen our resentment towards the judge.

The agony of living under judgment makes human lives tragic. We spin our wheels in avenues of escape. As the Psalmist writes: "Whither shall I flee from thy presence? If I ascend to heaven, thou art there! If I make my bed in Hell, thou art there!" (Ps. 139:7-8). We can choose to resist judgment openly and heroically, perhaps for a time victoriously. But whether it be the implacable forces of criticism and cruelty stemming from other people and our own inner selves, or whether it be the demand of God for perfection, judgment is in the end too strong for us. As Job finally answered the Lord, "I know that no purpose of thine can be thwarted" (Job 42:1). We can choose to appease the destiny of judgment. We can open negotiations. But that, too, is never enough. The judge will not be satisfied by anything we do. "No human being will be justified in God's sight by works of the Law" (Rom. 3:20). Moreover, appeasement will always feel compulsory; it is always accompanied by anger. The forces of judgment are too inbred within the historical life of humanity and too tenacious within ourselves to be defeated by one of these strategies. The result in each case is defeat: defeat by default in the case of escape, defeat with honor against insuperable odds in the case of open resistance, and defeat by surrender in the case of appeasement. It is defeat, in every case.

The strategies we create to meet our fear are natural to our humanity. They are profoundly understandable. Each one needs to be regarded with compassion. None of us has failed to use some of them; most of us have used all of them. But the universal result is defeat. I wish we could get around this. The problem of being human, which is to be at the mercy of hostile forces before which we feel unworthy and ashamed, has not been resolved. We have neither been able to resolve it nor to make peace with it. Even accepting our fate will not reconcile us to it; acceptance proves inadequate because of the sheer mammoth scale of human misery. The misery persists in disturbing the most stoic calm. We cannot cope with the pain. It seems deeply fitting to cry out with Saint Paul, "Who will deliver us from this body of death?" This is humanity's cry of dereliction.

II

Who Will Deliver Us?

TEARS are a precious measure of the things that really matter to us. Some experiences have an almost universal power to evoke tears. Weddings, for example, touch strong emotions in many of us. The bride and groom are leaving their families to make a new home. Their leave-taking can be sufficient in itself to bring up every feeling we have ever had about having or not having a place in the family. Weddings touch upon the intense, complex love existing between parents and children, and the aspirations we all have for lasting mutual love. Weddings touch upon our wish for a secure place in a home of constant love.

Funerals, too, evoke tears. Even if the service is religious, with the promise of peace in an eternal home, our deepest feelings relate to loss. We are sad because the person we loved is gone.

Again, the birth of children evokes tears. We are touched by the defenselessness of an infant, perhaps because a part of us feels defenseless. We are filled with hope, especially if our present seems somber, because a new life has begun. As the parents, we will try to create a home for the child, a place of nurture and reassurance. The coming of a child can be unforgettably affecting.

When my wife suffered a miscarriage at fourteen weeks, I was overcome with grief. As I drove from the hospital on the day it happened, I wept for the baby and for the home it would never have with us. I wept at the unbearable thought that we could ever lose the two children we do have. I wept for myself and for my wife in the loss we had suffered—for its pathos and disappointment. The loss was symbolized for us in the maternity bathing suit my wife had needed at the beach. When we hung it back up in the closet, it was enough to trigger every feeling of loss and separation we had ever had, as well as every wish for security and reassurance.

Tears disclose our need for a home. This aspiration exists deep within our nature. Margaret Hamilton, the actress who played the Wicked Witch in the beloved film *The Wizard of Oz*, told a journalist that she still cries when she sees the film: "Whether the home was happy or not, a situation or circumstance or four walls, that theme of going home is the universal thing in us" (*New York Times*, 27 August 1981). The need for home is so much a part of us, in fact, that any threat to it can shake us. This is why judgment provokes the fear it does: for it assaults whatever fragile security we may have achieved. It undermines our hope for a secure home. Tears measure this hope for a home as well as the universal doubt that we shall ever have one. Tears are a clue to the root of fear and the overwhelmingly negative effect of judgment in our lives.

The overwhelmingly negative effect of judgment points to the deep root of our fear: fear of nonbeing. Put simply, this is the suspicion that our worth, when all is said and done, equals precisely nothing. We suspect that if all our façades were taken down, what would be seen is no more than a trembling shadow. The fear of nonbeing comes frighteningly to the surface in situations in which we feel discarded or discounted. Perhaps a woman has been married for twelve years. She discovers that her husband has deceived her. His infidelity is no short-lived episode, but a trail well covered, cutting through every day of several years. When she finds out, he leaves her for another. The lawyer for the abandoned wife confides to her, "Now you know you've been put on the ash heap." What is the cruelest aspect of this? It is her feeling that she has been regarded with contempt, cast off as if she did not exist. This is possibly the most hurtful thing that can happen to us, to be treated as valueless. It confirms the worst fears we can harbor about ourselves.

Survivors of the Holocaust write that the most horrifying memory of the death camps is the experience of being treated as an animal, being regarded as subhuman. From the moment a Jew was herded onto the train bound for the concentration camp, he was treated like a beast to be slaughtered. He was fortunate if he were kept alive for a time because of some expediency on the part of his captors. This subhuman regard, which was a maintaining principle for the entire system of death camps, was the most bruising thing about them, the factor that could convert overnight a prisoner's outlook into one of total enervation and spiritual suicide. Ultimately, judgment touches the deepest fear of humanity: that we may have no inherent right to exist.

There is another case of tears to consider. These tears point to a moving but most unlikely release from fear. They are evoked by sacrifice.

Few writers have been able to move us more with the idea of sacrifice than Charles Dickens, in the last chapter of *A Tale of Two Cities*. In Dickens's story, Sydney Carton carries his love for Lucie Manette to the extreme length of sacrificing his life by taking the place of her husband, Darnay, on the guillotine. He conspires to have Darnay drugged and smuggled out of prison the night before he is sentenced to die, and returned home to his wife (Carton's true love) in England. He then disguises himself as Darnay, takes his place, and is executed the following day. As he ascends the scaffold, Carton weighs his action: "I see the lives for which I lay down my life, useful, prosperous and happy, in that England which I shall see no more. I see Her with a child upon her bosom. . . . I see that I hold a sanctuary in their hearts, and in the hearts of their descendents, generations hence. I see her, an old woman, weeping for me on the anniversary of this day. I see her and her husband, their course done, lying side by side in their last unearthly bed, and I know that each was not more honoured and held sacred in the other's soul, than I was in the souls of both. . . . It is a far, far better thing that I do, than I have ever done; it is a far, far better rest that I go to, than I have ever known." This is a parable of one man's sacrifice for the sake of love.

Such a sacrifice as Carton's helps us approach the ideal of atonement. To be atoned for means to be freed from a judgment by means of a sacrifice coming between us and the judge. The problem with atonement is that *everything depends on the value of the sacrifice* as measured by the judge. If the sacrifice is insufficient in value, the judgment remains in effect.

Every atonement includes a sacrifice. Sacrifice is the means by which atonement is able to happen. But atonement implies a further condition: removal of guilt. Atonement implies that the first party in the transaction is in a position of actual guilt in regard to the judge, and that the sacrificing agent assumes this guilt. It is not only a matter of a person's interposing himself by sacrifice between another person and his negative destiny. Essential to atonement is the perception that actual guilt and consequent judgment have estranged the two parties. The power of atonement derives from its removing guilt from the situation.

We need to be careful with the word *guilt*. It has bad associations. In the minds of many people, guilt is identified with repressions of pleasure, burdensome obligations, and irritating duties. It has almost assumed the meaning of "false guilt" or "neurotic guilt," guilt that is just in our minds. If we are to measure the profundity of atonement, we need to restore *guilt* to a reputation of respect.

On the one hand, Webster's Dictionary defines guilt in objective terms: "the fact of having committed a breach of conduct, especially such as violates law and involves a penalty," or "culpability." That is to say, guilt is a state, objectively measured by a given standard, of having done wrong, hence deserving judgment. This definition restricts itself to conscious guilt, guilt we carry because of conscious acts of wrongdoing. We can accept this definition of guilt as far as it goes. If I, for example, being a believer in God, break one of the Ten Commandments and am fully aware that I am doing so, I may be able to acknowledge my guilt after the fact, even if other considerations proved sufficient in the act to overrule the voice of conscience.

The problem with this description is that guilt is not simply a conscious thing. It is also an unconscious thing. Guilt inhabits a larger sphere within our lives than just conscious moral decisions. For example, if I feel I have to work ten hours on homework every Sunday night in order to prepare for Monday's class, I have a right to ask, Why am I doing this? The more so do I have such a right if I am aware of hating the assignments and dreading the Monday class. Why do I wreck my Sunday in order to do something I hate? The answer is probably something like "to get an A so as to qualify for medical school" or "to get an A so as not to disappoint my parents."

Whenever we do something we do not like, regardless of whether it is an "objectively" good thing for us to do or not, we can ask, Am I acting out of guilt? Am I discharging a debt? Am I trying to attain an end in order to please someone who would be upset with me if I did not attain it? Evidently guilt is an element in more than just conscious moral decisions. It is a universal element in all the efforts we have ever made to win approval.

Because of our universal need to win approval, hence to stave off judgment, the idea of atonement holds great appeal.

In the Bible, an atonement is a sacrifice by means of which the judgment we experience is assumed by another—a lamb or a dove or a person—with the result that we are not only freed from judgment but reconciled to the judge. This can evoke tears. It symbolizes our desperate hope of being lifted out of the pit of fearfulness. It signifies a release from the dereliction of fear that neither escape, nor open resistance, nor appeasement have yet been able to win for us.

The concept of atonement is an element in many of the world's religions. But there is little confidence in the history of religions that atonement has ever actually been made. We witness many attempts to make atonement and little confidence of lasting success. What we see, rather, is a setting up of systems of atonement in a hundred thousand forms, which are temporary in effect and need to be repeated. The problem is always this: The success of an atonement depends on the adequacy of the intervening sacrifice to satisfy the judgment of a hostile force. In most world religions the hostile force is a god. Unless the sacrifice is able to satisfy the demand of the god, it will be discounted. Judgment will go on. Atonement will need repeating.

In ancient Israel this was the bitter and ever-recurring story of the people's national life. Year after year they sacrificed to God for their sin; they put forward atonement in acknowledgment of their failure to satisfy God's demand for holy living. The Book of Deuteronomy describes a system of annual scapegoating, for example, by which the sins of the people would be transferred symbolically, through the hands of the high priest, to the head of a goat. The people would then harass the goat out of the city into the wilderness, their sins being dismissed with the goat. The system of Temple sacrifice developed later, with its aspiration of creating ways and means of atonement to satisfy the righteous God. Lambs and doves without blemish could suffice to draw off his wrath.

Other voices in the Old Testament, however, criticized these systems of sacrifice and atonement. The prophets protested that they were ineffective. The people were not experiencing freedom from guilt. The sacrifices had to be repeated year after year. They did not put judgment to rest. And the people heard the word of the Lord, "I will accept no bull from your house, nor he-goat from your fold. . . . If I were hungry, I would not tell you; for the world and all that is in it is mine. Do I eat the flesh of bulls, or drink the blood of goats?" (Ps. 50:10, 12-13). In other words, do the people think that a bull or goat will satisfy the One who owns the cattle on a thousand hills?

Added to this was the burden, which the people felt oppressively, that their inward lives and thoughts, as well as their outward actions, remained year after year fearful, devious, and self-justifying. They were in a terrible bind. They, like we, desired an atonement. But nothing they could do seemed acceptable. They understood themselves as guilty and willful despite their best renewed efforts to solve the problem.

The need and ideal of atonement is a familiar theme in many religions. More than ten years ago it burst over me in a fantastic manner when I was required to sacrifice a goat. It was the first day of the season for a large archaeological excavation in Turkey. We were uncovering an ancient city that had been a center for classical sculpture in the late Hellenistic period. The village men who supplied the work force were nominal Muslims. The site, however, had been associated for centuries with fertility worship. The "spirits of the hill," as they were known, were still believed to be active. The men feared that our digging would anger the spirits. So every year on the first day of the season, the custom was to slit the throat of a goat—to ward off, in advance and explicitly, the anger of the spirits. The Europeans on the staff would draw straws for this disagreeable duty. Mine that year was the short one. I slaughtered the goat as the foreman held its head firmly between his hands. Then we were all required, European staff and village laborers, to stand by and watch, until the goat was still. Only then could we disperse. Atonement had been made: We could begin the dig in peace.

Every year this had to be repeated. For every year that we took out our maps and measuring lines to recommence the work, one of us would be required to sacrifice a goat. For the villagers' sake we could *never* neglect the ritual. It was a living illustration of a tragedy referred to in the New Testament: "In these sacrifices there is a reminder of sin year after year. For it is impossible that the blood of bulls and goats should take away sins" (Heb. 10:34).

Humanity's search for atonement is not restricted to explicit religious acts. In the world of religion, atonement is offered to satisfy the judgment of the gods. In the secular world, atonement is offered to satisfy the judgment of others: persons, communities, institutions, and ideologies to which we feel responsible. The guilt, the judgment for falling short, is in reference to different objects, but *in both worlds it functions the same*. In personal relationships, for example, we can find ourselves seeking atonement by means of "good deeds." Perhaps we have neglected someone who was once a valued friend. We are reminded of this and feel guilty. We then perform a good deed for the person we neglected. But the good deed looks out of proportion given our earlier silence. It reeks of guilt. The intended recipient knows this; we know it. Does reconciliation occur? Rarely.

In the context of children and parents, a man once told me that he had achieved his considerable success at work in order to satisfy his parents. But he had no joy in this. He wrote, "I realize that I've tried to sacrifice for my mother. So she'll die relatively happy about her son – and I'll be ruined." Whether it is religious or secular, guilt can issue in high achievement. It can issue in service to others. But does anything we do ever absolve it? Can we ever rest?

Atonement may be an impossible ideal. We need it. We wish for it. In its poignancy we respond to it with tears when it is expressed symbolically in a story like *A Tale of Two*

Cities. Instinctively we know with the biblical writer that "perfect love casts out fear" (1 John 4:18). We know that perfect atonement would end our fear of judgment. But where is it to be found? "Who shall deliver us from this body of death?"

We are in a place of tragic solitude. We have identified the fear of judgment as the tragedy beyond all tragedies. Strategies have occurred to us for facing this tragedy: strategies of escape, strategies of open resistance, and strategies of appeasement. We have observed the disappointment inherent in each of them. Not one of them is able to succeed in resolving the problem.

We have now caught a glimpse of another strategy, perfect atonement. Atonement takes on the irresistible force of guilt. Going further than appeasement, atonement presents a hope of fully satisfying our judges. But even as we have been dreaming of an atonement, we have still found ourselves in a place of tragic solitude. This is because we cannot locate an object — even if it should be the sacrifice of our own life, let alone our life's hopes and aspirations — capable of satisfying our judges in a lasting, decisive way. The success of atonement as a means of healing our fear depends entirely on the value of the sacrifice as weighed by the judges. If it is insufficient to satisfy them, the atonement fails. Have we ever located in ourselves or in anyone else — or for that matter in any possibility we can conceive — an object to serve as our perfect atonement? Reality requires us to end this chapter in a mood of devastated idealism.

III

"Christ Died for Our Sins"

A verse from the first chapter of John's Gospel speaks directly to our tragic failure to find atonement. "No one has ever seen God; but the only Son has made God known" (John 1:18). Whether God cannot be seen or will not be seen, he is, simply, not to be seen. At exactly this point of reality, however, John adds, "The only Son has made God known." Referring to Jesus Christ, John places all his hopes on a single development, something he believes has changed everything.

John speaks for the human race. We are bound up in a universal tragedy, our failure to find an answer to fear. We have sought escape, resisted openly, or tried to appease. We have scoured our lives and loyalties for an atonement. Nothing costly enough has been found. We would gladly give the name of God to any successful instrument of escape, resistance, appeasement, or atonement. A successful instrument to free us from fear would seem divine. None has been found.

For this reason, John, in placing all his hopes on one person as the unique disclosure of a universal answer, sets the stage for an almost chilling anxiety of commitment. If only the Son has made God known, then the hopes of humanity rest upon the Son. This needs to be spoken in a hush, because it evokes a hope that if disappointed will mark the last stage of despair. Hope in the Son is a last resort. If the Son has *not* made God known, and if we agree with John that no one has ever seen God, then we shall remain in a place of tragic solitude. There is nowhere else to go. It is either solitude, mankind utterly disappointed at the end of a final, shattering search for an atonement that cannot be—or a question of all our hopes placed upon a solitary figure.

Walker Percy, the novelist, has described humanity as "waiting for news." Christianity says that the news has come. It brings to the human situation the news that what we most need has been supplied: perfect atonement for guilt. It declares that what we know to be true about ourselves has been responded to decisively and eternally from outside ourselves.

This confidence that there is good news for humanity in the place of our solitude is summed up in the words "Christ died for our sins." What do they mean? First, they refer to a man born in an obscure province of the Roman Empire during the reign of the Emperor Augustus, a man whose life was of such a character that he became known as the "Christ," that is, the "Chosen One" or "Messiah" who was to "save the people from their sins." Second, the words say that he died: he was crucified in humiliation by the Romans. Third, the words link his death directly with our sins: he suffered because of them. The implication of this is that he died in our place, in some sense standing in for us at the bar of judgment. Potentially at least, "Christ died for our sins" is a statement of infinitely large value.

What is the present value of the death of Christ? How can something that happened long ago meet the judgment that afflicts us now? We have proposed that the problem of being human is essentially a factor of fear. We live our lives under judgment. Whether it is for wrongdoing in a conscious mode or the pervasive, irrational, multiform fear that we are worthless and no good, we live our lives under judgment. Saint Paul's way of stating this is that humanity is under law. In no state does humanity exist without reference to law, that is, accusing authority. In Paul's frame of reference, law is embodied ideally in the Law of Moses, the Law from God. But he stretches the definition of law to include the inner voice of self-accusation that exists in all of us. In either case, whether it is expressed in the Ten Commandments or in the judgments of others and our inner selves, law cannot correct us. The fear it stimulates makes our attempts to obey it ever more edgy and desperate. In fact, the harder we try to live up to the law, the worse we feel about our failure.

Paul believes that what law is unable to do, God has done in Jesus Christ. He writes, "God has done what the law, weakened by the flesh, could not do: sending his own Son in the likeness of sinful flesh and for sin, he condemned sin in the flesh, in order that the just requirement of the law might be fulfilled in us" (Rom. 8:3-4). We can paraphrase his logic this way: Human nature has proven inadequate to the task of meeting the judgment under which it staggers to survive. Rather than controlling us, let alone elevating us, judgment strangles us.

But, says Paul, God has intervened. He has sent his Son, in the form of a human being, and has let fall upon him the full force of the judgment that makes our own lives miserable. The full requirement of law has been met and paid. Humanity is free from judgment.

This needs enhancement. Like us, Paul feels deeply the dereliction of fear that is our destiny under law. The only way Paul can conceive of this destiny being changed from a universal, tragic, unalterable script is for law to be fulfilled with lasting effect. No wonder, then, his exultant shout of triumph at the end of chapter 7 of the epistle to the Romans, "Thanks be to God through Jesus Christ our Lord" (Rom. 7:25). Paul understands that law was laid to rest forever by the death of Christ. The whole oppression of judgment, in every sense and every mode, has descended upon "the Son in the likeness of sinful flesh." This descent of law for all time upon the head of another spells the end of law as a power to deal death to humanity.

In his "thanks be to God through Jesus Christ our Lord," Paul is convinced that the sacrifice of Jesus Christ on the cross is of unique value in fulfilling the law. For one thing, Jesus is the Son of God. He is loved by the Father within a unique relationship. This gives birth to the amazing thought that the Father and the Son could, in a focus beyond time and space and human reason, agree to the death of the one, beloved to the other, in the interest of freeing humanity from fear. "When the time had fully come, God sent forth his Son, born of woman, born under the Law, to redeem those who were under the Law, so that we might receive adoption as sons" (Gal. 4: 4-5). Humanity's destiny is of such importance to God that he makes a costly sacrifice to effect an end to our oppression.

Moreover, Paul believes that Jesus Christ is God. "He is the image of the invisible God. . . . For in him all the fulness of God was pleased to dwell" (Col. 1:15, 19). This conviction takes away the appalling possibility that the death of Christ could have been cruel or capricious, the Father punishing his innocent beloved Son so that we, the guilty, might be exonerated. Rather, the atonement is a transaction from God to God. God visits his justice upon himself.

Furthermore, Jesus' divinity endows his sacrifice with eternally satisfying value. The only one who can fulfill God's demand—implicit in his nature—for perfection is God himself. Hence in judging Jesus Christ to death in our place, the principle of law is both terminated and vindicated. It has done its worst. It has prosecuted its standard to the furthest possible limit, meaning death to the lawbreaker. This is why we can say with Paul that the death of Christ marks the end of the law (Rom. 10:4).

Paul's "Thanks be to God through Jesus Christ our Lord" reflects one further conviction. This is the conviction that Jesus was raised from the dead on the third day. The resurrection of Jesus makes it possible to be joyful about his atoning sacrifice even when the sacrifice has resulted in his suffering and death. For Paul and the whole early Christian movement, the sacrifice on the cross has present efficacy, inspires present joy, because Christ rose. "We know that Christ being raised from the dead will never die again; death no longer has dominion over him. The death he died he died to sin, once for all, but the life he lives he lives to God" (Rom. 6:9-10). The empty tomb carries the atonement into an eternal present. Hence "we also consider ourselves dead to sin and alive to God in Christ Jesus" (Rom. 6:11).

For all of Paul's telescoping theology, we can observe in his letters something else about him that is crucial. We observe that the starting point for his theology is personal experience. For Paul the problem of fear, which has gripped him in common with the rest of the human race, has been resolved. From a connection forged between his personal bondage to fear and the fact of Jesus' death on the cross has come his conviction of atonement. And from this conviction has come his ideas about the being of God, the identity of Jesus, the present availability of forgiveness, and the hope of eternal life. All these ideas develop for Paul from his experience of the human tragedy resolved. His personal conviction of atonement is the soil for the characteristic emphases of Christian theology.

In his letter to the Philippians Paul talks about his own experience in reference to Christ's sacrifice. He talks about himself: "[I was] as to righteousness under the law blameless. But whatever gain I had, I counted as loss for the sake of Christ. Indeed I count everything as loss because of the surpassing worth of knowing Christ Jesus my Lord. For his sake I have suffered the loss of all things, and count them as refuse, in order that I may gain Christ and be found in him, not having a righteousness of my own, based on law, but that which is through faith in Christ, the righteousness from God that depends on faith" (Phil. 3:6-9).

I believe in the atonement of Jesus Christ because it disarms the law and frees me from the fear of judgment. This judgment would use as evidence against me not only the deliberate sins and conscious moral failures of which I feel most painfully aware, but also the compulsive patterns and imprisoning proclivities the origin of which I scarcely know except they feel like flesh of my flesh. I have often felt judgment not as the condemnation of things about me I can help, but condemnation of my very self and character. Judgment makes me believe that "I," to the extent that I am able to think of myself as a unity, have no definite, rightful place in the world. Because of judgment, I feel in the position of having to earn this rightful place. I have always worried that the governing truth about my life may be the dark finality of grievous solitude. Do I have a right to exist? The law has judged not only what I do, but who I am. For this reason law is my chief adversary in life.

I am a little like the duck hunter who was hunting with his friend in a wide-open barren of land in southeastern Georgia. Far away on the horizon he noticed a cloud of smoke. Soon he could hear the sound of crackling. A wind came up, and he realized the terrible truth: a brushfire was advancing his way. It was moving so fast that he and his friend could not outrun it. The hunter began to rifle through his pockets. Then he emptied all the contents of his knapsack. He soon found what he was looking for—a book of matches. To his friend's amazement, he pulled out a match and struck it. He lit a small fire around the two of them. Soon they were standing in a circle of blackened earth, waiting for the fire to come. They did not have to wait long. They covered their mouths with their handkerchiefs and braced themselves. The fire came near—and swept over them. But they were completely unhurt. They weren't even touched. Fire would not pass where fire had passed.

The law is like the brushfire. I cannot escape it. But if I stand in the burned-over place, where law has already burned its way through, then I will not be hurt. Not a hair of my head will be singed. The death of Christ is the burned-over place. There I huddle, hardly believing yet relieved. I believe in the atonement. The law is powerless: Christ's death has disarmed it. "Thanks be to God through Jesus Christ our Lord!"

IV

...Doth Make Heroes of Us All

THREE weeks after the birth of her baby, Betsy released her child for adoption. She was unmarried and had no job. The child's father was out of the picture. Betsy's giving up her baby was a heroic action. Soon after, Betsy, alone now, wrote this: "In allowing Susan to be adopted, God has invited me to further trust and growth in faith. I accepted the invitation when I signed the papers for her release. I heard my own heart break when I did so, but I have faith in the balm of his hand to heal me."

"I heard my own heart break." The words are tragic. They convey sorrow deeper than words. At the same time, they convey her grief so honestly that Betsy appears to be a hero.

If a transition were possible in human experience from lives devoted to unsuccessful strategies attempting to overcome fear, to lives of heroism and trust, then many of us would be interested. If it were really possible to make a move from cowardice to heroism—and not because of duty, but because the roots of cowardice had been dug up, exposed, and withered, and it was no longer necessary for us to be cowards—then many of us would try. I believe the atonement of Jesus Christ has made such a transition possible. It has absorbed the force of conscience, which "doth make cowards of us all," and satisfied its unyielding demands. It has put away the Damocles' sword of condemnation. Both vindicating the rule of law and terminating it, the atonement has opened a route to freedom that points to the possibility of heroism in human lives. The atonement of Jesus Christ exists to make heroes of us, in place of cowards.

When she released her baby for adoption, Betsy heard her heart break. Yet she said she had "faith in the balm of his hand to heal me." How could such pain coexist with her heroic action? How was this strange coexistence possible for her, or for any of us? I believe the atonement is at the heart of it. We shall now consider the impact of the death of Christ on a single life —even our own. This is an issue on which Christianity rises or falls as a practical religion. How can the atonement of Christ touch a single human life? If it can touch one, perhaps it can touch a family's life or a people's life.

The healing process opened up by the atonement can be expressed in the phrase "assimilation of negativity." The healing agent is imputation: attributing a characteristic to someone that he does not have by nature. The result of healing is integration, an end to the splits that divide and conquer us. To a greater or lesser degree, integration issues in heroism. Although these terms sound abstract, they relate momentous good news to us in our bondage to fear. They signify an actual possibility of change in the midst of the givenness and inertia of ordinary living. Spoken to the human situation that we have called a dereliction of fear, and in the light of a historic, effective atonement, these terms bear good news.

Consider the phrase "assimilation of negativity." This means taking in or embracing, as part of one's conscious self, the sadness, disappointment, and dark side of experience. It is the opposite of splitting. Splitting is the phenomenon of distancing our conscious self from unacceptable feelings and experiences to such an extent that a fissure opens between the conscious self and the unconscious self. Whether psychoanalysis is right or not in suggesting that splits develop in us from earliest infancy, the sufferings of which separate repressed from conscious memories, we know for certain that splitting occurs inside us every day. Something bad happens and we wish it away, or hide it, or rationalize it. For example, we can hear bad news and literally refuse to believe it. A man can be told he is being fired from his job. He can be told in the most direct possible language that he is being dismissed. But when he takes the stand at the hearing scheduled on his behalf, he claims in all sincerity that he did not take what he heard to be exactly what it was: news of dismissal. He could not hear it. Certainly he could not bear it.

Everyone is capable of this. We take great pains to avoid painful truth and when we have no other choice but to stare it in the face, we still deny it, rationalize it, or contend against it. Splitting is natural to us when the pain of life comes close. But splitting is unsuccessful. It divides the self. It forces us into speaking, seeing, and hearing with more than one set of perceptions. It serves to create a hell of either/or, by which experiences are either acceptable and good (that is, minus suffering) or unacceptable and bad (that is, only suffering). Many of us find ourselves shuttling back and forth between the different sides of our splits. Manic depression is an extreme form of this movement; it exists in an infinite number of gradations.

Assimilation of negativity is a way of describing what happens when the unbearable experiences of our lives are brought within the mainstream of our conscious selves. It is another way of saying realism. Realism has never been a mean achievement. It is a hard-won asset. And it differs from cynicism, with which it is sometimes confused, by only a slender thread —the thread, I believe, of God's grace. Assimilation of negativity refers to a person's willing, painful embrace of the sorrows of life, of himself and his flaws, in coexistence, almost union, with his confidence, aspirations, and joys. We are thinking of the person who can say, on the one hand, "I am an incredible idiot," and at the same time, "Life is good and the future holds out hope."

We could almost refer to this assimilation of negativity by the terms *perspective* and *maturity*. Certainly the union of self-knowledge and hopeful effort has defined maturity in more than one culture and era. But the death of Christ offers an instrument of unique value in making possible such a union. If the assimilation of negativity implies the marriage of absolute realism to active hope, how can such a thing be possible, given the intense, static nature of humanity's sufferings? How can we assimilate our negativities in all their grievousness without being overwhelmed by them? Here the atonement speaks with power.

A phrase from Martin Luther maps the way of assimilation. The phrase is "at the same time justified and a sinner," or, simply, "justified *and* a sinner." The phrase emerges from Luther's theology of justification by faith, which he in turn learned from the New Testament. The phrase declares that a Christian is one who is both "justified" in God's sight, that is, regarded by God as just or Law-fulfilling; and a sinner still, that is, susceptible to and driven by the same compulsions that have always been with him. "Justified and a sinner" devastates with one shock any notion that a Christian is not a sinner. On the contrary, it states bluntly that he is both a sinner and a righteous person, at the same time. It implies a radical assimilation of negativity. How can this be? It sounds like a paradox. But it leads us straight to the question of leverage, the means by which Christianity makes possible the healing integration of realism and hope.

The key to integration is the removal of judgment. For it is judgment that forces us to split. The atonement of Jesus Christ has removed the Damocles' sword of judgment that has been overshadowing our lives. For us, the way to experience this end to judgment's reign—the end of the Law—will be the dynamic concept of *imputation*.

Imputation is a theological concept well illustrated by an analogy from life: Alfredo was a Mexican peasant boy whose parents, brothers, and sisters had all died in a fire. His face had been burned badly, almost beyond recognition. He used to wander over the countryside, begging for food and scavenging from refuse heaps. By age twelve he had become a local legend, half village idiot, half untouchable.

His existence became known to a priest who administered an orphanage for boys in the region. Sometimes from a long way off, Alfredo would watch the boys playing soccer. One day the priest strode out of the great iron gate of the orphanage and towards Alfredo, who was sitting, watching, on a nearby hillside. The priest put his arms around the boy, who was terribly suspicious, and asked him whether he would come to the orphanage if a place could be found. Not believing his ears and half-expecting a trick to be played on him, Alfredo said yes. The priest added that he would have to ask the boys first, warning that they might cause trouble and say no. If they said no, the priest would not force it.

That night the priest summoned into the courtyard all the orphans, mostly teenaged boys. He came out to address them, Alfredo accompanying him warily from behind. The priest announced to the boys, "This is Alfredo. You know who he is. Will you have him in our school?" There was a long silence. Alfredo felt the stares of two hundred pairs of eyes. He knew how ugly he was. There was a long silence. Then the head boy stepped forward. He looked straight into Alfredo's eyes: "Alfredo, you are one of us." That night Alfredo was taken into the orphanage.

To impute means "to treat as if." It means to regard a person *as if* he or she had such and such a value or quality, although intrinsically he or she does not. It is the assigning of worth to someone who would not otherwise have such worth. Expressed in the language of Christian theology, imputation is the crediting in our favor, from the standpoint of God, who is the source of judgment, of the perfect moral worth of Jesus

Christ on the cross. Conversely, imputation implies the humiliation of Jesus Christ at the moment in time when he died, by means of the transfer to him of the full burden of human sin that is normally, universally accounted to us. This is a cosmic moral transfer, involving infinite credit assigned to us and running thoroughly against the facts as we experience them; and infinite discredit assigned to him, running thoroughly against the facts as God knows them. Imputation, this moral transfer running against the evidence, is expressed economically and precisely in a sentence from 2 Corinthians: "For our sake he made him to be sin who knew no sin, so that in him we might become the righteousness of God" (2 Cor. 5:21).

This is a staggering idea. It has implications of great practical importance for lives and cultures. But before we consider its implications, it requires enhancement. We need to remember that humanity is working, in the last analysis, from a position of tragic solitude. What Paul means by sin is a position of failure over against God. Although the Law was conceived by God for our good, humanity's fear of condemnation from that Law has so absorbed our attention that we have found it impossible to obey from the heart without benefit of compulsion or control. Our confidence has been drained away by failure. We are compelled to fear; we reckon ourselves inadequate and frail in the extreme.

Now we hear that God has identified Jesus, his perfect Son and self-expression, with our dereliction. For early Christianity, Jesus' cry from the cross, "My God, my God, why hast thou forsaken me?" was crucial. It spoke of Jesus' unreserving identification with the tragic solitude of humanity. The early church came to believe that Jesus had died in humanity's place, the "just for the unjust" (1 Pet. 3:18). In doing so, his perfection, what we have called his perfect moral worth, was transferred to us universally and conclusively. Our sin, the confining, compulsive bondage to fear that results in innumerable symptoms or sins, was transferred to him for a blinding, eternal moment. The effect of this is that God has created a new humanity, humanity "in Christ," who are identified with the moral perfection of Christ. Hence for Paul, "If any one is in Christ, he is a new creation; the old has passed away, behold, the new has come" (2 Cor. 5:17).

The concept of imputation, of a cosmic moral transfer of infinite worth to us at infinite cost to God, is profound because it does justice to our human nature as it really is. It understands God as possessing an incentive to love by which he overlooks the symptoms of our tragic captivity, regarding us rather as perfect through the lens of his Son's sinless humanity. The enabling power of the transfer rests in the eye of the beholder, God, whose appraisal is the only thing that ultimately matters. We are speaking of God's "reckoning us dead to sin and alive to God in Christ Jesus" (Rom. 6:11).

At the same time we ourselves continue to be flesh and blood. We are neither lobotomized nor morally disinfected. We are the same persons we were. But there is more to it than that. In being regarded righteous, or reckoned as having infinite worth (literally "worded," to use Bible language—see Romans 4:3, Galatians 3:6), we are by God's *fiat* truly so, in a way beyond all appearances. It is not a legal fiction. To interpret imputation as legal fiction would mean "God says, 'I know you are rotten but for reasons of my own I choose to regard you as perfect. But just between you and me, you're still rotten!' " Imputation does not mean that. Rather it is the case that just as God once said, "Let there be light" and there was light, so when he says, "Blessed is the man to whom the Lord imputes no iniquity" (Ps. 32:2), this state of blessedness is true in actuality.

How does it work out? How does the strange mix of perfection imputed and fear still experienced settle in a person's life? What does a person look like who is "justified and a sinner"? Consider any chronic problem a person may have. The more personal or "close to home" the problem is, the harder it is to admit about ourselves. If it is a sexual compulsion, it could threaten our career and family. The same is true of an addiction. Perhaps it is a secret from the past, the knowledge of which would, we are convinced, destroy others' image of us. Perhaps it is a sorrow related to our life's circumstances, such as the death of a parent or sibling when we were young or our spouse's sudden death after just a few years of marriage. Our sorrow may have defeated us at a deep level. We may be living life as if we were just going through the motions, self-pitying and angry. It is impossible to assimilate the negativities.

Enter the news that God imputes righteousness to us. We are in a different case than we thought. We have nothing ultimately to lose from our afflictions because God looks through them and beyond them to see the perfect humanity of his Son on the cross. Because we are not condemned by the power of ultimate judgment in the universe—quite the contrary, for he has yoked the affliction to himself—we do not need to condemn ourselves, or parts of ourselves, in our weakness and defeat. We can enter the unfamiliar territory of honesty, hence of unity. We are justified in God's sight, needing no longer to be split off from our fear and its effects. We are all sinners because we know we are still in a sense the same. We do not have to be surprised at the stubbornness and perseverance of compulsive fear. But we are different, because in being regarded as righteous, we start to become as we are regarded.

In order to illustrate this, we can contrast the responses of two different people to affliction. Kate, for example, works in the advertising business and seems single-minded in regard to her work. She takes her job so seriously that it looks like the only thing in life that matters to her. We suspect, in fact, that her near mania about the job hides fears and needs within her. She confides that her hyperactivity alternates with depression, depression so deep that she has to miss at least two weeks of work every year because of it.

Kate is a member of a prayer group. No one in the group is unaware of her mania nor of her depression. Nor, on the other hand, would we wish to "confront" Kate with the "truth" about herself. Rather, we are hoping that in time she will find through us enough care from God to face the fact of her manic oscillations. After eighteen months of trust slowly building, Kate tells us one night how truly desperate she feels. She has erected one defense after another, she says, all of them in the interest of warding off the bitter fact that she is chronically depressed. The job has been her most effective, lasting defense. But even the job no longer drives away depression.

Because she is a Christian and thinks that Christians are not by definition supposed to have emotional problems, Kate has always perceived God standing in judgment over this problem she has not been able to name, let alone control. The breakthrough for Kate occurs in her trusting the prayer group enough to come to a point of honesty about herself. She puts into words something like, I am depressed. I need help. Here is the freeing self-definition, "I am a sinner," a kind of repentance, the radically uncharacteristic but necessary breakthrough of honesty. Here, too, is an occasion for Kate to hear the word, "But I am also justified." It will be a mediated word, through human beings, we hope through us to whom she has disclosed herself. We will seek to regard her, for ourselves, as confident because she is not condemned, serene because she need not fear, patient because her need for love has been met.

I know Kate well. It has been three years since the thaw. She is no longer alienated from herself, that is, from her suffering part. She has become married and is as successful in her work as she used to be, although it is not so much the striving thing it was. She can even begin to speak, cautiously, about the love of God, for which her friends have been present messengers.

Another person's struggle with negativity offers a disturbing contrast to Kate's. Anne was living with Tim for a couple of years while both of them practiced law in the city. After a difficult period between them, they separated. Hurt more painfully than they had expected, each resolved to start a new life. But Tim could not keep away from Anne. Nor could she resist when he called. So began a year of blissful returns, followed by excruciating separations, four, five, six cycles of this. Although each was convinced that the problems between them were too big for them to consider marriage, the sexual and emotional tensions when they were apart were more than they could bear. How long could this draining conflict go on? The most difficult problem with Tim and Anne was not, in fact, their bitter cycle of return and regret. It was their inability to be honest about the situation.

Anne, too, was in a prayer group. Although she would sometimes refer to "confusion about relationships," she could not call the problem by name—a sabotaging obsession she was visiting upon herself, over which she had no control. She could almost call the problem by name in the setting of one-to-one counseling: "I know it will never work with Tim; I am exhausted. But part of me almost seems to enjoy it." Anne was afraid the prayer group would reject her for her captivity to the affair with Tim. Because she could not share the problem in trust with other people nor with God in any meaningful sense, she had to split.

Anne is still leading two lives. Integration is not possible for now. In fact, she carries a ruthless contempt towards the split part of her that relates to Tim. This is a situation that may not change until Anne's fear subsides enough for her to hear that God, as well as her sincere friends, regard her as beloved in spite of her self-contempt.

The precious gift of self-acceptance because of God's regard is given in several incidents from the life of Jesus. For example, a Gentile woman came to Jesus when he was preaching in the northwest corner of Palestine. She asked him to heal her daughter. After stating that he came "only to the lost sheep of the house of Israel," he added, "It is not fair to take the children's bread and throw it to the dogs." She replied, in a combination of daring and humility, "Yes, Lord, yet even the dogs eat the crumbs that fall from their masters' table." She was willing to be known as "a dog," that is, accept his interpretation of her religious status, in the setting of a personal meeting. She was willing to accept his judgment, painful and humbling as it was for her. On the other hand, Jesus' reply to her words of acceptance bore an astounding affirmation, "O woman, great is your faith. Be it done for you as you desire" (Matt. 15:27-28). Her daughter was healed instantly.

The woman had humility and, in the setting of the ministry of Jesus and its strategy towards the Jews, amazing honesty. She accepted Jesus' derogation of her as a dog. Within it she could still ask for his help. We are close to the classic idea of repentance. In light of the presence of Jesus, which we can infer to have been gracious despite the limits he set in words, she was able to hear and receive his perspective that she was a "Gentile dog." It was heard and taken in. From within it she was able to find her famous words, richly commended by Jesus, that "even the dogs eat the crumbs from their masters' table." This woman assimilated her negativity in the context of the regard of Jesus Christ.

The same experience is depicted elsewhere in the New Testament. With the Roman centurion, another Gentile, there is this same convergence of daring and abasement. On the one hand, the centurion was a man of authority whose orders were always obeyed. On the other hand, he called his authority cheap in comparison to Jesus': "Lord, I am not worthy to have you come under my roof; but only say the word, and my servant will be healed." Jesus marveled, "Truly, I say to you, not even in Israel have I found such faith" (Matt. 8:5-10). In like fashion the woman with the issue of blood (Matt. 9:18-22) was able to approach Jesus both shamelessly and ashamed, "justified and a sinner." Shamelessly she pressed through the crowd to touch his garment; ashamed she could not address him in words because of her degrading chronic history of uncleanness. Yet he said to her, "Take heart, daughter; your faith has made you well."

Other examples from the New Testament include blind Bartimaeus of Jericho, who had no scruples in forcing himself on Jesus' attention. At the same time he was laconically honest about his need: "Son of David, have mercy on me! . . . Master, let me receive my sight." Jesus replied: "Your faith has made you well" (Mark 10:46-52). There was Mary Magdalene, ashamed and in tears, loving much because she had been forgiven much (Luke 7:36-50). She had the abandon to approach Jesus in the house of a Pharisee, crashing through a taboo in order to express her thanks. Here is an amazing unity of courage and remorse.

A virtual summation of "justified and a sinner" occurs in Jesus' words to the woman taken in adultery, which are found in the Gospel of John. Jesus had deflated the self-righteousness of her accusers as they faced her in the Temple when he said, "Let him who is without sin among you be the first to throw a stone at her." The accusers having crept away in chagrin, he "looked up and said to her, 'Woman, where are they? Has no one condemned you?' She said, 'No one, Lord.' And Jesus said, 'Neither do I condemn you; go, and sin no more' " (John 8:10-11). He justified her first in not condemning her, and added, "sin no more." He both forgave and acknowledged.

Stories like these, in the New Testament and today, demonstrate imputation. Jesus' righteous regard enables us to see ourselves in truth and accept the truth. Admission of our bondage and consequent pathos, in light of his regarding us through the lens of ascribed moral perfection, terminates the natural process of splitting. Our new impulse can be honesty, in hope of healing. From our perspective we can express the experience of imputation in these words: I am what I am, yet I am also what He is. Or to draw from the First Letter of John, "We may have confidence for the day of judgment, because as he is so are we in this world. There is no fear in love, but perfect love casts out fear. For fear has to do with punishment, and he who fears is not perfected in love. We love, because he first loved us" (1 John 4:17-19).

Imputation is the transfer of moral perfection to the account of our humanity. (This humanity would, if left to itself, experience life, to the contrary, as anxious slavery to fear.) It is commonly mediated through imputing persons. It is the work of God because, as Saint Paul writes, "We are ambassadors for Christ, God making his appeal through us" (2 Cor. 5:20). Whether it is mediated through imputing persons in the here and now or whether it is described as unmediated affirmation on the part of the unseen God, it is ultimately a mediated experience in every case, insofar as "the Word became flesh" in Jesus Christ. The leverage of the cross in human affairs is the righteousness of Christ imputed to us. It is the divine seeing of ourselves through the lens of the substantial and divine perfection of the Son. We are "justified *and* sinners."

Being justified by the instrument of imputation, we are, moreover, enabled without fear to examine honestly the scars of fear, hence to assimilate them. Honesty in the light of radical mercy confers upon lives a virtually noble quality of daring. This is Christian heroism. It is the combination of hope with truthfulness, which is sufficient to deflate the element of self-righteousness in our well-doing while not retarding the urge to act out of hope. We have the necessary ingredients of a Christian theology of healing and integration.

A poetic description of Christian heroism occurs in Kierkegaard's *Fear and Trembling*. Kierkegaard's words capture the lack of pretense or surface attainment—the normality—of the assimilation of negativity offered by the atonement. At the same time he sees the infinite worth and precious rarity of assimilation.

"This man has made and every instant is making the movements of infinity. With infinite resignation he has drained the cup of life's profound sadness, he knows the bliss of the infinite, he senses the pain of renouncing everything, the dearest things he possesses in the world, and yet finiteness tastes to him just as good as to one who never knew anything higher. . . . He constantly makes the movements of infinity, but he does this with such correctness and assurance that he constantly gets the finite out of it, and there is not a second when one has a notion of anything else. . . . To transform the leap of life into a walk, absolutely to express the sublime in the pedestrian—that only the knight of faith can do—and this is the one and only prodigy" (*Fear and Trembling*, [Garden City, N.Y.: Doubleday, 1954], pp. 51-52).

V

Massacre of the Innocents

DESPITE the integrating principle of imputation to bring to life Christ's atonement in an age of depression, there is an unsolved mystery bound up with it. This is the mystery of innocent affliction. Nothing is more puzzling nor more likely to ignite our anger than the suffering of innocents. Nothing is more likely to make us doubt God than innocent affliction and its virtual universality in human experience.

Innocent affliction takes as many forms as there are people — then many more among families, groups, and nations. In the case of individuals, we are talking about abandonments, deprivations of love, and conflicts in loving, which children may experience from birth. Homes can be deserts of indifference or hatred, where the need of a child to be cherished is unmet or frustrated by conflicting emotions from and between the parents. It could be something as simple, and ghastly, as the mother whose inverted nipple, unknown to her, makes it impossible for her baby to receive milk during the first days after birth. A doctor discovers the problem and helps rectify it, but only after twelve days of the child's famished screaming and failure to thrive. It could be something as subtle, and voracious, as a father's jealousy of the infant who has just been carried home from the hospital in the arms of its mother, his wife. For now, father will have to take a backseat. He cannot stand this. So he becomes an adversary to the child and induces guilt in his wife.

In another situation, does it help us understand the "touch-me-not" attitude of a friend, her committed reserve in never talking about herself, when we find out her mother died when she was born? The psychologist Harry Stack Sullivan said, "Everyone is much more simply human than otherwise." Experiences of affliction produce effects in all of us. No one is immune to suffering. Many of our rough edges and sheer unhappinesses are related to unasked-for sufferings from the archaeology of our personal pasts. Many of us grow up with scars too deep to be seen.

Consider, too, the brute fact of human malevolence visited upon innocent people. Consider Herod's slaughter of all the children in Bethlehem after the birth of Jesus: the massacre of the innocents. "A voice was heard in Ramah, wailing and loud lamentation, Rachel weeping for her children; she refuses to be consoled, because they are no more" (Jer. 31:15). Consider the Holocaust of modern times. Nothing can add to nor detract from the horror of the death camps, the bestiality and scale of the evil. Nothing can add to it nor detract from it. Elie Wiesel's well-known description of the hanging of a Jewish youth in Auschwitz expresses the unfathomable evil of the camps: "The SS hanged two Jewish men and a youth in front of the whole camp. The men died quickly, but the death throes of the youth lasted for half an hour. 'Where is God? Where is he?' someone asked behind me. As the youth still hung in torment in the noose after a long time, I heard the man call again, 'Where is God now?' " (*Night*, [New York: Avon, 1972], p. 75).

Resignedly, in words for all time, the Roman Stoic Marcus Aurelius states the problem of the persistence of wickedness: "What is wickedness? It is that which many times and often you have already seen and known in the world. And so, when anything happens that might otherwise trouble you, let this thought come to your mind, that it is something you have already seen and known. Nothing is new." We have mentioned the accumulating evil and injustice caused by man's inhumanity to man. There are other categories of innocent affliction to consider. There is the sharp prominence of natural catastrophe and random disaster. Think of the destruction of Pompeii in A.D. 79 or the Lisbon earthquake of 1755 or the annual devastating floods in India. The list of natural catastrophes in history is very long, with literally millions of victims. Add to this the plagues and epidemics that have wiped out peoples and cities and towns: whole villages of American Indians dying from smallpox imported by Europeans, whole populations in France and Germany wiped out by the Black Death in the fourteenth century. How can a God of justice and mercy allow these things to happen? The question rises up in all of us, from the stratum of our psychic deserts of love, which we did not create; to the level of "man's inhumanity to man"; to the insoluble puzzle and extreme revulsion created by the randomness of disaster, accident, and sickness visited upon us all.

A further category to consider is the particular suffering experienced by religious people, and not just randomly as is our common destiny, but in the full light of faith in God's mercy. Poignant, even ironic, is the suffering that the New Testament writers, for example, believe Christians will undergo on account of their faith. In the Gospels Jesus confides to his disciples, "Take heed to yourselves; for they will deliver you up to councils; and you will be beaten in synagogues; and you will stand before governors and kings for my sake, to bear testimony before them. . . . and you will be hated by all for my name's sake" (Mark 13:9, 13). "If they persecuted me, they will persecute you" (John 15:20). There may be a clue in these predictions to the scandal of innocent affliction, a clue drawing us to the innocent death of Jesus on the cross. In any event, the words are an unguarded confrontation with a disturbing aspect of innocent suffering: Believers in God are not exempt from, but all the more liable to, the invasions of inhumanity and innocent affliction.

Innocent affliction is a striking challenge to faith in a God of justice and mercy. To put it bluntly, How can a God of justice and mercy permit evil to exist and flourish unchecked in a world he has made? The question is more than an intellectual one. We all have our grievances against God. On a Sunday morning at church we had a class on the persecution of Japanese Christians in the seventeenth century. This persecution virtually wiped out the Christian church in Japan for two hundred years. After the class a thoughtful person commented, "It makes you question the providence of God." There was no response to the comment; there is no answer to it. At every level the existence and extent of innocent affliction force us to question the providing love of God. We can voice the resignation of Saint Paul: "We know that the whole creation has been groaning in travail unitil now; and not only the creation, but we ourselves, who have the first fruits of the Spirit, groan inwardly as we wait for adoption as sons, the redemption of our bodies" (Rom. 8:22, 23).

As in earlier chapters, so now, the experience of suffering, in particular the suffering of innocents, brings us to a place of grievous solitude. There is a basic question at the center of our experience that cannot be answered. Its lack of an answer is the more hurtful for religious people. Religious people claim to know a God who relates himself to them. Innocent suffering, both in the abstract and in individual existence, can prompt a severing of this relationship: It makes us want to cut our ties and turn our backs on God.

Any hope of resolving this will have to rest on some kind of reconciliation inside ourselves with the perverse omnipresence of innocent suffering. Somehow, if we are to live with and in the midst of innocent affliction, we require a means, as before, of assimilating the negativity. With innocent affliction just as with fundamental fear, flight will not work.

Nor will confrontation. Nor will appeasement. Will the death of Jesus Christ help?

A clue appears in an essay by the late English psychiatrist Frank Lake, who was also a Christian. Speaking of innocent affliction experienced by infants as early as birth, Dr. Lake wrote: "No blame can attach to the parents for most abnormal deliveries. It is not so, to the new born, denied an early opportunity to experience the mother's tender nearness. The failure of any human being to answer the urgent appeal for a presence gives rise to a deep inner horror of a 'god' who is dead, perhaps killed. The reproach re-echoes in the mind and still reverberates as a pervasive heartbreak. A basic question of [the source of evil] is avoided only by the infant's attributing the badness of the unbearable situation to some inexplicable but indelible badness in its own very being. This is the usual outcome. It is unthinkable that 'the gods' are bad. Far better take the blame and leave *their* [italics added] righteousness intact. Parents are too powerful to dispute their handling. But we Christians have a God who 'is so near to us' (Deuteronomy 4:7): he is both the crucified God and the God who absconds from himself. . . . This, says Luther, is the *deus theologicus*, and the principle of our knowledge of him crucified is shot through with paradox and contradiction" ("The Work of Christ in the Healing of Primal Pain," *Theological Renewal*, No. 6, June/July 77, page 9).

The death of Jesus speaks to our speechlessness before innocent suffering in at least three modes. One mode is to share our suffering with us. The crucified Jesus is by definition a sharer in the absolute abandonment and pain of sufferers. He bears the yoke of pain with us. This is a contention of the New Testament: "It was fitting that he, for whom and by whom all things exist, in bringing many sons to glory, should make the pioneer of their salvation perfect through suffering. . . . Since therefore the children share in flesh and blood, he himself likewise partook of the same nature. . . . For because he himself has suffered and been tempted, he is able to help those who are tempted" (Heb. 2:10, 14, 18). The writer contends that in our suffering we can be armed by the confidence that Christ also suffered unjustly.

An illustration of the ministry of Christ's sharing our pain comes in an eyewitness account of a martyrdom of Japanese Christians in October 1613. "After the Martyrs were all bound to their pillars, the Christians [i.e., the bystanders] lifted up aloft, for the Martyrs and all the rest to look and meditate upon, a very devout picture of our Blessed Saviour as he was bound to a pillar. Then the souldiers putting fire unto the wood and straw, the Holy Martyrs in the middest thereof with all devotion called upon the help and favour of their Blessed Saviour often tymes, to that end naming the most holy name of Jesus, and all the Christians, upon their knees did sing the *Creed*, the *Pater Noster, Ave Maria*, and other praiers untill the Martyrs had given their Holy soules into the hands of God" (C. R. Boxer, *The Christian Century in Japan*, [Berkeley: University of California Press, 1974] p. 342). In their agony the martyrs looked upon a picture of Jesus in agony.

For believers, the confidence that Jesus bears innocent affliction with them can bring comfort. In the same period, for example, of persecution in Japan, manuals on martyrdom circulated among the faithful contained a single thought that was repeated over and over: "While being tortured, visualize the Passion of Jesus" (Boxer, p. 354). The Book of Hebrews states this same confidence of solidarity: "For we have not a high priest who is unable to sympathize with our weaknesses; but one who in every respect has been tempted as we are, yet without sin. Let us then with confidence draw near to the throne of grace, that we may receive mercy and find grace to help in time of need" (Heb. 5:15-16). This text has been quoted down through the centuries for purposes of encouragement and consolation among believers under persecution.

For all its consolation, however, God's making common cause with humanity's pain in the death of Christ is at best a partial response to the enormity of innocent affliction. For one thing, it is a consolation only for believers. It is not going to comfort a person in the midst of random suffering who is not a Christian. Even for the Christian it has limited efficacy. It does not help us understand why. Why is this happening to me? to my family? to my people? The death of Christ as a sharing of pain does not justify God to man. It does not right the wrong. It is of limited help to us when we are face to face with the vastness of evil and affliction in our own lives and in human history.

On the other hand, the New Testament does not set out to answer the why of injustice in the world. Jesus said the same rain falls on the just as the unjust: the wise man who built his house upon the rock endured the same storms as the foolish man who built his house upon the sand. Jesus and his followers promised neither a present end to suffering nor a definite answer to why it exists.

Nonetheless, there is a second ministry that the death of Jesus brings to the pain of innocent affliction. It is the ministry of acknowledgment. The death of Jesus acknowledges the ongoing reality and striking power of injustice. Theoretically, God could have arranged it so that Jesus did not have to die ignominiously. "Do you think that I cannot appeal to my Father, and he will at once send me more than twelve legions of angels?" (Matt. 26:53). But God did not do this. Jesus died alone, in shame and humiliation.

This is an unfathomable acknowledgment on the part of God to the persevering affliction of pain and suffering in the world. It is a ministry to the givenness of innocent affliction. Granted, Jesus says in the Gospel of John: "In the world you have tribulation; but be of good cheer, I have overcome the world" (John 16:33). Believers *can* take heart that Jesus rose from the dead, signaling the ultimate end of the force of evil. But in its heart the crucifixion reflects the seriousness with which God takes the universal presence of innocent suffering.

God concedes to it and bears the brunt of it in the death of Jesus, which is the death of God. In his living and dying God acknowledges that "in the world you have tribulation."

Within this acknowledgment, there is again no answer to the question of why he did not arrange matters differently. Given the omnipotence of God, why did he not re-create the conditions of existence and annihilate evil? That is the question for which we are given no answer. All we can say, perhaps, is that in conceding to suffering, God at the same time provided for transcendence and victory in the Empty Tomb, providing by means of it the promise of a future, decisive, and eternal end to sorrow. "New Jerusalem" is the New Testament's picture of a kingdom without tears. It will be established in the future.

Acknowledging our innocent affliction embodies a response to it. It means we are forced to face it squarely. Here Christianity is at its most realistic. Do other philosophies of life offer the awesome paradox of an ancient equivalent to the electric chair planted on the most exposed, public, and praising part of its edifice? What other philosophies flaunt the most appalling symbol of injustice in front of everything else? God's taking innocent suffering seriously is demonstrated in an extreme way by the palpable symbol of the cross. In the extremity of God's own dereliction lie the seeds of overcoming. It suggests that God is asking the same question we ask: "Why?" He is asking the question in the most direct way love can ask it, by laying himself on the line. The point is offered in the conclusion of Elie Wiesel's account of the hanging of the Jewish youth at Auschwitz. "The older men, forced to watch, groaned with sighs too deep for words, 'Where is God now?' And I heard a voice in myself answer: 'Where is he? He is there. He is hanging there on the gallows' " (*Night*, p. 75).

Christianity does not promise resolution in present time to the pervasive question of innocent suffering. We hear that Jesus bears our suffering with us, that he crowds into the water with sinners when he is baptized by John, and later cries out our cry of forlornness, "My God, my God, why hast thou forsaken me?" The words can exist as consolation to believers in the midst of pain. We hear that in the death of Jesus God concedes to the besetting challenge of innocent affliction by laying himself open to it. Jesus' expiring on the cross *is* the question. We can almost say, God is asking the same question we ask, and in a way so concrete that our abstract debates about the origin pale in comparison. But another question goads us: Is the injustice ever righted? Even if the resurrection declares the ultimate victory of justice and mercy over evil caprice, is present injustice ever righted? With this question we are led into a third response voiced by the cross to the mystery of unfairness and pain.

In an earlier chapter we spoke of a person who at unbearable cost to herself gave up her baby for adoption. Even though she believed in her head and we felt in our hearts that she had done the right thing, nothing could make up her loss. She could arm herself with the thought of the rightness of the action. Her courage was in itself a nurturing affirmation for her. And the fact that her baby was in a loving, sustaining family proved of real comfort to her. But even in the best of worlds, Betsy had lost her baby. Once she was sobbing desperately in the company of a friend. The friend sympathized, "I realize how hard this is for you. You've had to tear out your heart. And nobody ever tore out their heart for you." Betsy protested, "Yes they did! God did." She was talking about the death of Christ.

This remark is a pathway, however dark and narrow, into a response of God on the cross that we shall refer to as discharging a debt. God discharged a debt on the cross to the victims of innocent affliction. He tore out his heart by giving up his son—himself—to right the wrongs of injustice under the shadow of which the world languishes.

The notion of God's discharging a debt can be inferred from the Bible, as in "Surely he has borne our griefs and carried our sorrows" (Isa. 53:4). But it is a theme induced primarily from experience, cast in the light of what Scripture says about the generosity of God. In a 1943 symposium entitled "What the Cross Means to Me," Charles Williams developed the possibility that God had discharged a debt by means of the death of Jesus. Williams began by stating that Christ recompensed the Holy Innocents whom Herod slew: "He too perished innocently." Williams continued, in a reflection valuable enough to be quoted at length, "This has seemed to me for a long time the most flagrant significance of the cross; it does enable us to use the word *justice* without shame—which otherwise we could not. . . . Our justice condemned the innocent, but the innocent it condemned was one who was fundamentally responsible for the existence of all injustice. . . .

"We are relieved . . . from the burden of being naturally optimistic. 'The whole creation groaneth and travaileth together.' If we are to rejoice always then it must be a joy consonant with that; we need not—infinite relief!—force ourselves to deny the mere burden of breathing. Life (experience suggests) is a good thing, and somehow unendurable; at least the Christian faith has denied neither side of the paradox" (Charles Williams, *The Image of the City* [London: Oxford University Press, 1958] pp. 133-34).

The two key sentences for us in Williams's reflection are "[The cross] does enable us to use the word *justice* without shame" and "Life (experience suggests) is a good thing, and somehow unendurable; at least the Christian faith has denied neither side of the paradox." Given the innocent affliction that shoots through our personal and social histories, we would indeed be ashamed to use the word *just* to describe God, were it not for God's being ashamed of himself. God's shame, God's humiliation at the horror of mass injustice, is manifest in his shameful, humiliating death. Not only does he tear out his heart by giving up the person most precious to him, but in that person he gives up his good name and reputation. This is enormously important. It is his good name that believers have sought to protect against the slurs of humanity's just grievance. It is not the job of Christians to maintain idealized attributes of God in the face of experience that calls them into question. God is other than he has been defined. To put it another way, God is principally defined by his shame and dereliction on the cross.

Several years ago some seminarians were visiting the machine shop of a men's prison in the English Midlands. The humming and banging of the machinery were the harsh background to any conversation. The seminarians stopped to speak to a prisoner. He glared at them and demanded an answer to the great question: "Well, vicars, how do you expect me to believe in a god who made the world such a bloody mess?" Anything they tried to say was stammered out, and drowned out in any case by the machinery. Truly at a loss for words, they left. Later the chaplain at the prison, an old hand, volunteered what his answer might have been. To the man in the shop he would have replied, "I don't believe in that god myself." The students, having wished to defend God's honor, were pulled up by the roots and amazed. What god *could* they speak of except a God who takes injustice seriously? The cross is the ultimate concession to injustice, in eternal terms a restitution for it, and, as earlier chapters have said, a fulfilling of it.

These words of Job contain a truthfulness with which we are forced to speak—even as they are uttered in the light of what Christians affirm about the providing love of God. "As God lives, who has taken away my right, and the Almighty, who has made my soul bitter; as long as my breath is in me, and the spirit of God is in my nostrils; my lips will not speak falsehood, and my tongue will not utter deceit" (Job 27:2-4). This is the best we can do, it is a very great deal, and it is also not enough. We have to live with it. Christianity promises many things. It promises above all else peace and joy in believing: It promises freedom from judgment, hence from fear. It promises joy in the present because the future is secured. It does not, however, promise exemption from sorrow and pain.

Quite the contrary, it pleads suffering as its center. It asks us to drink the cup of suffering, yet not as masochism but as the means of transcending suffering by conceding to it within the providing care of God.

The atonement of Jesus Christ displays God sharing our sorrow. It displays God conceding to innocent affliction. It displays God discharging a debt to suffering innocents by sacrificing his dearest love. God pays for his own allowance of evil in the unimaginable death of his son, himself. We cannot say more than this. We do in fact see through a glass darkly. But we place the cross at the top of our spires to declare that our unendurable pain is not forgotten.

VI

Atonement
in the Church

THE good news of atonement has great implications for the
Christian church. There are challenges it compels us to take
up and challenges from which it relieves us. What we say
about the death of Christ shapes our message and conditions
our ministry. His death judges the church in order to reform
it. It excites us to renew it. This chapter seeks to challenge the
church in an age of depression with a word and ministry
shaped by the death of Christ.

The cornerstone of a ministry based upon his death is the
concept of justification by faith. We would wish to preach it
ahead of anything else. Justification implies the desperate problem of nonalignment between God and humanity that is summarized by the phrase "dereliction of fear." For the fear to
end, guilt must end. For guilt to end, atonement must be
made. For this to happen, God alone can be responsible. That,
we believe, he has been, in the death of his Son. Justification
by faith tells us that we cannot hope to shoulder by ourselves
the burden of guilt. It is infinitely too burdensome for humanity to carry.

Fortunately, the church is able to say that our guilt has been
borne in full by the perfect one, Jesus of Nazareth. "For our

71

sake he made him to be sin who knew no sin, so that in him we might become the righteousness of God" (2 Cor. 5:21). Underneath this is a condition of either/or: Either we are perfect or we are guilty. Since we are evidently not the former, and since the latter relegates us to a solitude to which extinction would be preferable, we are caught in a trap. The death of Christ rescues us. He became nothing so that we might have everything. This is reflected in another text from 2 Corinthians, again an astonishing either/or: "For you know the grace of our Lord Jesus Christ, that though he was rich, yet for your sake, he became poor, so that by his poverty you might become rich" (2 Cor. 8:9). Justification gives us everything because it understands Christ to have exchanged with us for a moment in time the hell of nothingness. In him, therefore, in his perfection exchanged to our credit, we have fulfilled the Law. The spell of the ought is broken.

A ministry based on atonement holds together two contrasting ideas: The Law is good and powerful, yet only one has obeyed it. We uphold the Law but acknowledge the depressing weight it places upon the humanity of all. Our ministry does not derogate the Law. It does not "lower the market," that is, lower the standard of the Law in order to accommodate our inability to live up to it. Lowering the market is a natural tactic in humanity's coping with the righteousness of God. We can see why church people, for example, have sometimes wished to underplay the Law of God, to soften it and find ways to conciliate our bitterness over its radical insistence. A ministry of justification by faith does not lower the market. It recognizes the tragic opprobrium of guilt, yet offers relief because news has come of an atonement provided by another. The Law has been satisfied. In the crucified we ourselves have satisfied the Law as well as the internal laws of our own personal narrative. We have crossed the border into a new country, a place of freedom from fear.

Rising out of the doctrine of justification, which is itself rooted in the doctrine of atonement, is the crucial concept of imputation. Imputation is crucial because it draws the blood of Christ into real situations.

Imputation has leverage on the problem of being human because it assures us that our value is infinite while at the same time relieving us of the burden of having to prove it. The claim is that God imputes, or reckons to our credit in his eyes, the moral perfection of his Son. This reckoning is without regard to our intrinsic faults or merits. Rather, it is a factor entirely of the moral perfection of Christ. Paul calculates the infinitely precious value of imputation in the fourth chapter of Romans. He is referring to Father Abraham, whose faith, in Genesis 15, was "reckoned to him as righteousness." "The words, 'it was reckoned to him,' were written not for his sake alone, but for ours also. It will be reckoned to us who believe in him that raised from the dead Jesus our Lord, who was put to death for our trespasses and raised for our justification" (Rom. 4:23-25).

A ministry of imputation calls for preaching and teaching a dramatic affirmation of the self. It is initially a question of recognizing a virtually universal negative experience of life: that we allow others to carry our value. Other people have an extraordinary hold over us: their view of us, or what we think their view is, matters more than what we think of ourselves. Imputation turns this situation around, declaring that in the great transaction of the death of Christ, God has reaffirmed the priceless value he conferred on human beings in our creation.

For imputation to be received, honesty is required. Although it is an overused word today, *honesty* is a fitting synonym for what the Bible calls repentance. Honesty is a truth-telling about our experience that has given up on strategies of flight, appeasement, or confrontation. Honesty means facing up to a tragic situation. In the New Testament, honesty is exemplified in Paul's confession that his righteousness, his claim to moral superiority—let alone integrity—in the face of judgment, is equivalent to garbage (Phil. 3:8). In the light of such honesty, God's imputation to us of Christ's moral perfection is a precious gift. It conveys authentic worth to personality. It is the root cause of what we have called Christian heroism.

A pastoral approach based on imputation can be differentiated from other approaches to ministry. For example, some ministries in the history of the church have been based on infusion. Infusion is the idea that God endows us with moral worth by conveying it to us so that it becomes ours inherently. If, having been baptized, we have entered inherently into a state of grace, then the baptism of water has conveyed something like an infusion. We are better inherently or ontologically after baptism than we were before. If we should fall into sin, we would fall out of the state of grace and need to be restored to it.

The distinction between imputation and infusion can be subtle. It is in effect a question of how the church deals with continuing sin in believers. Imputation, because it writes the script from God's point of view, implies that the believer remains "justified *and* a sinner." Infusion, because it writes the script from humanity's point of view, suggests that a person is either "justified," in the state of grace, *or* a "sinner," needing restoration. On this view, *justified* and *sinner* cannot describe the same person at the same time.

A notorious difficulty with infusion is its tendency towards self-righteousness. Let us say, for example, that I am involved in the charismatic renewal. I have been taught that when I am able to speak in tongues or evince one or more of a specific catalogue of spiritual gifts, I am entitled to believe I have been baptized in the Holy Spirit. Should this occur, I am almost bound to believe that the Spirit has blessed me more than somebody else who has not had the experience. The idea of a second blessing makes the Spirit of God into a quantity. It suggests that something has been infused in me that does not exist inside another. I have been given a license to judge. Classic Pentecostal teaching implies such a doctrine of infusion. Imputation, on the other hand, leaves the matter up to God, claiming for humanity the fullest conceivable mandate—God looks upon us as being in Christ, hence perfect—and conceding at the same moment our shattering dereliction of fear that makes us feel as if we were worth nothing.

A ministry based on imputation has at least two definite consequences. First, it believes the ancient Greeks were correct in identifying the goal of life as "Know Thyself." Some self-knowledge is a prerequisite in experience for hearing God's word of grace. My friend Diana, for example, is overweight. She covers up the inner problems to which her weight gives a clue by means of compulsive talking. She gravitates to Christianity as a religion of infusion. She is reassured to hear that all must receive Jesus Christ as personal Lord and Savior to dwell within them. Her religion provides her deep stratum of anger with an object: the others, the ones who will not believe in Jesus. Add to Diana's background a Pentecostal experience of Spirit baptism during her adolescence, and link to that her upbringing in a conservative church where the sacraments were described to her in terms of infusion, and we have a case of religion shoring up the fortifications that stand between this woman's pain and any chance she might have to receive love. Fortunately for Diana, other life circumstances have been building momentum: she is under stress from other quarters. Her sexuality, for example, is a mystery to her. She wonders if she is gay. She certainly is tempted to act out in ways that confuse her. She confides to a prayer group that she is not what she seems. She is fast approaching a crisis and is asking for help.

Diana is in the process of repenting. She is coming to a place in life where her fortifications of defense no longer serve her. She is coming to a point of admitting her solitude. When she gets to this point, she may be in a position to hear that her worth was established by God at the cross and is reckoned in the present. This word may have a chance to get through to a wounded, broken, honest woman. Diana may be able to hear the word of God's applied righteousness in a way that will turn the negativity of her pain into an occasion of hope and praise.

A second consequence of a ministry based on imputation is that it regards sanctification, or Christian growth, as a function of justification. What this means is that growth is the process of receiving God's word of justification in new areas of our being. It is the carrying of good news to the unevangelized territories of our personal and social being. If justification is God's regarding us as perfect through the mirror of the Son's perfection, then sanctification, which is growth in grace, is our receiving that regard palpably and with larger and larger extension throughout the complex geography of our being. For Saint Paul, sanctification is this continuing process of receiving the word of imputation. The process is as long as life itself, reaching to darker continents within ourselves and our culture than we ever knew existed. Sanctification is justification by extension.

This picture of sanctification is in contrast to views of growth that offer new knowledge or new experience as the gateway to blessing. I think of Frank, who was baptized as an infant within the Episcopal Church, then confirmed at age fourteen. During his first year in college, Frank left the church and became an agnostic. At a point of crisis during his sophomore year, he had a conversion experience through an evangelical fellowship on campus. To mark this experience, he was rebaptized in a river. During his senior year he came under the influence of a friend in the charismatic renewal. He was baptized in the Holy Spirit and received the gift of tongues. After college Frank started a job. A slow process of disillusionment began. The more experience he had of life, the more suspect he grew of his experience in college. He eventually dropped out of fellowship. In his late twenties, however, an intellectual quest began to draw him to the work of writers who were traditionalist Roman Catholics. At age thirty, convinced that he had found the true church, he became a Roman Catholic. Had his search come to an end? Unfortunately, no, for at age thirty-five his marriage ended in divorce. When he wished to remarry four years later, he was rebuffed by his church. He decided, ironically, to return to the Episcopal Church.

How can we interpret Frank's experience, which is a composite portrait of many who search? There is often this desire in us for something more, something better and more immediate. This book claims that our search takes its origin, sustenance, and ultimate direction from *past* experience—the death of Christ. Progress in our lives is not principally a matter of new experience or new knowledge. It is rather a fresh returning, in every new round of events, to a very old conviction: Christ died for our sins.

In addition to preaching, teaching, and experiencing justification by faith and imputation, pastoral ministry that is rooted in atonement will emphasize another primary concept. This is providence. The ministry of atonement helps to build our confidence that things will be well in the end, that God will provide for his people. The doctrine of providence can be illustrated from the story of Joseph in the Book of Genesis. Joseph was sold by his brothers into slavery and taken to Egypt. Through a long series of incidents and circumstances, he went from being a slave in the house of Potiphar to principal agent for the Pharaoh. He amazed and mortified his brothers years later when, after they had traveled to Egypt to buy food during a period of severe famine, he revealed himself to be not only alive but in a powerful position. His words of reassurance to his brothers are a pure expression of faith in God's providence: "And now do not be distressed, or angry with yourselves, because you sold me here; for God sent me before you to preserve life. . . . God sent me before you to preserve for you a remnant on earth, and to keep alive for you many survivors. *It was not you who sent me here, but God*" (Gen. 45:5. 7-8, italics added).

This is the conviction of providence. It can transform the most sullen resentment. It is the long view that gives meaning to events that appear heartless or confusing. Consider a person who is fired from his job in midcareer. He is plunged into a harrowing crisis of confidence. Years later he looks back: he sees that he lost a job but found his faith. A woman is jilted by the man she had determined to marry. All is lost. Years later she come to believe that the man walked out of her life so that she would find her best love, the good man to whom she is now married. At the heart of injustice there is still a God who is good.

This is the conviction of providence. It is lifted up throughout the New Testament. A brilliant meditation on the providence of God occurs in chapters 9 through 11 of the letter to the Romans, in which Paul is puzzling, indeed weeping, over the resistance of his own people to the new messianic faith. Given the historic chosenness of Israel, Paul cannot understand why the Gentiles have been the ones, for the most part, to respond to his message. "My conscience bears me witness in the Holy Spirit, that I have great sorrow and unceasing anguish in my heart. For I would wish myself accursed and cut off from Christ for the sake of my brethren, my kinsmen by race" (Rom. 9:1-3).

Paul seeks to "defend" God against charges of caprice and unfairness. Why after centuries of chosenness has Israel not been given to believe in Jesus as Messiah? "What shall we say then? Is there injustice on God's part? By no means! For he says to Moses, 'I will have mercy on whom I have mercy, and I will have compassion on whom I have compassion.' So it depends not upon man's will or exertion, but upon God's mercy" (Rom. 9:14-16). The facts of Paul's ministry, so different from what he might have intended, compel him to ask, Why? He does not know the answer. What he does believe is that God is essentially merciful and that his mercy is witnessed on the cross. The intent of God at the end of the day is "that he may have mercy upon all" (Rom. 11:32).

Providence creates a positive outlook on life. It lets us know that in the midst of death we are in life. The writer to the Hebrews expresses it this way: "Be content with what you have, for he has said, 'I will never fail you nor forsake you.' Hence we can confidently say, 'The Lord is my helper, I will not be afraid; what can man do to me?' " (Heb. 13:5-6). This would be harmful nonsense and delusion were it not for the cross. Were it not for the death of Christ, God's atonement in the face of his judgment, and God's concession to the injustice of the very world he made, we would have no meaningful basis on which to be hopeful. Christianity goes back again and again to a source of hope that lies in the past: the death of Jesus as pledge of promise for the future.

A ministry based on atonement allows for an anchored trust. We do not underestimate the force and brunt of affliction. But we interpret our way through it by means of a secure hope that is anchored in the past. Providence puts the burden of hope on God. It does not expect too much from our personal exertions. Not much we do is likely to diminish the fear and suffering that exist so pervasively throughout our histories. But God, as the Bible never tires of saying, will keep us from falling. While we shall retain a healthy suspicion of ourselves, our efforts, and our motives, it is finally he who is "at work within us, both to will and to work for his good pleasure" (Phil. 2:13). God provides.

A ministry based on atonement carries at least three large implications for the practical functioning of the church in an age of depression. First, we shall preach and teach the same message to believers and nonbelievers alike. We will not discriminate between what we offer believers by way of good news and what we offer nonbelievers. This is basic, because it is almost universal in conservative Christianity that the church makes a definite distinction between its message to those inside the camp and its message to those outside. This distinction comes in the construct "Christian" vs. "non-

Christian," or "baptized vs. "unbaptized," or "saved" vs. "un-saved," etc. It is a false distinction in pastoral care because it fails to take into account that all human beings, believers as well as nonbelievers, live in the house of bondage to fear.

This is not to suggest that distinctions do not exist between believers and nonbelievers. Distinctions do exist—just ask a nonbeliever if he considers himself a believer. We do take stands that are different from other stands. That being the case, however, a ministry based on atonement does not assume that one person is in a better position *vis-à-vis* the bondage to fear than another. Our bondage is an extremely subtle, complicated thing. A person can have been a conscious Christian for ten years, and yet have very little idea of the extent to which he is living under compulsion. Conversely, a conscious non-Christian can have a more mature self-understanding, a truer perspective on his limits and ambivalences, than any number of Christians.

In our ministry we understand the whole of humanity to be in bondage to fear. Our message is simply for anyone willing to hear it. For most of us, Christian growth will involve an enduring, painful missionary advance of the good news into areas of our lives that are still as bound as they were before. Bringing release to the captives is the ministry from us all to us all. We are not able to distinguish, from the vantage point of the Christian ministry, between categories of persons. The ministry of good news is for believers and nonbelievers alike.

A second implication of a ministry based on atonement is the warning it signals to self-righteousness. Indeed it confronts directly the basic human proneness to self-righteousness. Expressed positively, this means that atonement places the burden of salvation and help so utterly on God that no room is left for human pride of achievement or pride of possession. We have seen already that ultimately—after appeasement, confrontation, and escape have all defaulted in the face of anxiety—we have no room left for such pride. Now, having received the good news of atonement from a source totally outside ourselves, we can enjoy rather than chafe at the situation. True, there is no room for pride or possession of achievement, but it is true, also, that we live "as having nothing, and yet possessing all things" (2 Cor. 6:10).

Every school of thought in the Christian church is susceptible to self-righteousness. A pastoral strategy based on atonement cannot, given our fear and fragility, prevent the wind from blowing in the direction of self-righteousness. But we can say clearly, "God has done what the Law, weakened by the flesh, could not do" (Rom. 8:3). No matter what the point of view, political label, or point of origin may be, self-righteousness has, by virtue of the atonement, entirely lost its potency. The façade can come down.

A third implication of a ministry based on atonement will be manifest in our preaching. Under the sign of atonement, our preaching will be descriptive rather than prescriptive. This is to say that the preacher will have sufficient respect both for the dignity of his hearers and for his own inability to rescue himself (let alone others) from the dereliction of fear, that he will refrain from moralizing. Has not the verb *to preach* become synonymous in popular parlance with *to tell what to do*? But we have seen that humanity is entrapped by forces greater than ourselves. We are victimized by our fear and guilt. The experience of victimization runs so deep that it is actually cruel to address someone as if the solution were as easy as turning his head. Within a pastoral ministry of atonement, our common ground of affliction and compulsion, common to preacher as well as hearer, can produce compassion. Moralism is a perversion of the Gospel.

Preaching the atonement is a difficult thing. It consists in identifying the universal problem of bondage and then offering what God has provided. It both excavates and sheds light. It is the manifesting of the objective atonement of Christ to the painful points of entrapment and despair that we experience subjectively.

Naturally, though sadly, many of us think we want ethical

prescriptions from the pulpit, moral exhortations, calls to holiness. That desire is what the New Testament refers to as the "flesh." The flesh, or *sarx* in the Greek, is the natural human tendency to need to lord it over people. It refers to our need to establish our integrity and worth in the face of judgment that is both ultimate and temporal. The "flesh" makes us need to reassure ourselves we are OK by having something of our own to make us all right. Evidently, the Law serves the flesh if we can convince ourselves that we are fulfilling it, for then we can produce a positive value judgment on our lives. The preaching of Law meets the need of our flesh. This is tragic. It has hindered the ministry of the church and created pharisees. It creates the opposite of what we have been enabled to become.

A ministry based on atonement preaches only humanity's need and God's remedy. It offers, it does not burden. It seeks to eschew prescription. To describe humanity's sorrow and to proclaim God's Gift—that, and only that, is the order of our business. Hebrews 13:9 makes the point by means of a metaphor of foods that are good and foods that are bad for the body. "Do not be led away by diverse and strange teachings; for it is well that the heart be strengthened by grace, not by foods which have not benefited their adherents."

Depending on the local situation, pastoral ministry based on atonement can take many different forms. However, three questions arise from our theology that help to assess the form and program of a local ministry. These questions are critical. They not only help us to criticize the initiatives we take in specific settings, but they suggest the broad themes of any ministry that is undertaken to help free people from the dereliction of fear.

The first question is this: Does our ministry provide people with a quality of worship by which they can get out of themselves? This is crucial. As derelicts of fear, we are preoccupied with our own problems. We cannot help this. But if we can be enabled, just for an hour, just for a few minutes, to step outside ourselves, we inevitably see ourselves from a fresh perspective, in the light of the grace of Jesus Christ on the cross. Worship can be the fulcrum to new vision. It provides leverage on the inversion and introversion that are natural to us. Just repeating the words, for example, of a familiar liturgy within an atmosphere of confidence in God can have a health-giving effect. Praise confers vision.

The second question to ask of our ministry is this: Are we building up a family in which the wounds of the past can be salved and the new freedom won by atonement encouraged? Family—a group of people who are committed to the freedom of the derelict—is crucial. This family is not the ultimate subject of love. *That* is God in Christ, the living Word, whom the strategy will not cease to declare from the pulpit. But the family is the best mediation we have in present experience for making the love of God specific.

In one city parish the family takes the form of many small prayer groups, meeting regularly to support and pray for the members. They place the Bible at the center of the small groups—a living expression of the justification from God that provides the derelicts of fear with a place to stand, the lasting position of affirmation. At the same time they do not shrink from the "growth-group" aspect. They want to encourage, in the light of atonement, a relationship among the group that is searching and transparent. This is not to call for "instant sharing." It is not to encourage a kind of facile intimacy that carries the look of honesty but is really morbid. But it is to look for moments of truth, moments when a person can observe himself as he really is yet not shrink away, because in fact Christ died for him. The small group, oscillating between study of the Bible's accounts of our humanity in Christ and honest approaches to our defended fears and pain, is an expression of the family we need. It is absolutely necessary that we ask of our ministry, Does it provide people with a family to mediate the imputing grace of God?

The third question to ask of our ministry is this: Does it provide people with opportunities for counseling? Does it offer to our derelict humanity the possibility of a healing relationship, person to person, to *mediate* the love of God? "Experience has taught us that we have only one enduring weapon in our present struggle against [emotional pain]: the emotional discovery and emotional acceptance of the truth in the individual and unique history of our childhood" (Alice Miller, *Prisoners of Childhood* [New York: Basic Books, 1981], p. 3). This statement from Alice Miller, a Swiss psychoanalyst, could apply to many of us who are not diagnosed as mentally ill. It goes under the heading of the assimilation of negativity, the necessary step to healing and integration. Do I suggest that everyone needs counseling? I am not sure. Many of us have problems that have been "successfully" defended: our inner strategies to contain them allow us relatively stable, relatively purposeful lives. Many of us, however, find ourselves crippled by unassimilated negativities rising to the surface. Many of us will draw benefit from counseling. The scars of the past can be healed. The counselor can be a messenger of affirmation and nurture to the hidden fear, thus entering our world as a mediator of atonement.

Again in the parish in New York there are several professional counselors who work alongside the clergy. They become heralds of good news to the solitary places of fear, the unevangelized territories of our hearts. They may seldom mention the name of Jesus Christ. But as carriers of love to dark continents, they are missionaries. We find that as the grace of God imputed to us in Christ is preached from the pulpit, the inner fears and tragedies of our listeners rise to the surface even in the most "well-adjusted" people. The grace of God will produce an unmasking of the self by which needs that are unconscious to a person in day-to-day life rise to the surface. At this point the counselor comes to sustain the ministry of the Word. He becomes an active participant in the ministry.

Our ministry is rooted in the atonement. It includes three emphases: worship, to lift us out of ourselves and renew our perspective; small groups to provide a nurturing family for us as we grow; and opportunities for counseling as a bridge to past hurts and a means of healing old wounds.

The church has many members who know about the healing effects of worship. Many in the church also stress the importance of small groups to create family in an alienated culture and world. Again, many in the church champion the cause of counseling as leverage on well-established resistances that cover fear. For us, all these elements find their unity in the scarlet thread of the death of Christ. The death of Christ is the radical answer to the problem of human resistance to love. It implies an intractable problem on the part of humanity that only a miracle can solve. It declares a resolution by which justice is total yet wedded to mercy. It announces a resounding, eternal affirmation of the human spirit, yet in all its need, pain, and innocent affliction. It holds together concepts and experiences, such as justice with mercy and man's justification with his sinfulness, that humanity would typically divorce. It is a unitive concept, grounded in a historical event that stands as the marvelous basis for the taking into ourselves and our collective history of the most damaging truths of the human situation, and thus by assimilating them in the cross, transfiguring them and redeeming them. We preach Christ crucified, "the power of God and the wisdom of God. For the foolishness of God is wiser than men, and the weakness of God is stronger than men" (1 Cor. 1:25).